The Leaven Of Hypocrisy

What exactly does the Bible say about hypocrisy?

And how can we avoid it?

First Edition

Evelyn Jones

Table Of Contents

Chapter five:Jesus Offers Escape from Hypocrisy

Conclusion

INTRODUCTION

Are you a hypocrite?

Jesus Christ heavily condemns hypocrisy. He lambasted the Pharisees for being a hypocrite. They received a heavy penalty for the sin of hypocrisy.

The problem with hypocrisy is it is difficult to detect for the person committing it. If you are given a sense of discernment, reading the Bible should be enough for you to determine whether you are a hypocrite or not.However, in most cases, it takes another person to point it out to the one who is being a hypocrite.

You're probably thinking by now that you are not a hypocrite, that you are living an honest and pure life. Well, the truth of the matter is that "WE ALL HAVE BEEN A HYPOCRITE", including myself. Sadly, we commit this sin without knowing it or even if we already know it, we simply ignore hypocrisy.

Why do you look at the speck of sawdust in your brother's eye and pay no attention to the plank in your own eye? How can you say to your brother, 'Let me take the speck out of your eye,' when all the time there is a plank in your own eye? You hypocrite, first take the plank out of your own eye, and then you will see clearly to remove the speck from your brother's eye."

–Matthew 7:3-5 (NIV)

With these witty but also biting words, Jesus causes his listeners then and today to carefully examine their own lives. Are we going about accusing others of minor shortcomings when, in fact, we ourselves are ignoring our own behavior? If so, we are hypocrites. Once our hypocrisy is removed, then we are in a position to help others.

Unfortunately, one obstacle to the acceptance of Christianity that is often raised is provided by Christians themselves. Phrased in many ways, the core of the objection is, "If Christianity is true, why are there hypocrites in the church?" In other words, if Christianity is really supposed to change people, then why do some who profess to believe in Jesus set such bad examples? As you continue to read this book the following chapters will answer the "hypocrisy objection"

to Christianity. But first, let's explore the
definition and the signs of hypocrisy in general,
as well as in a biblical sense. As it is crucial for
us Christians to know the signs of a hypocrite.
By being familiar with these signs, we will be
aware of what to change in our lives and
become better followers of God.

Chapter One

The Biblical Meaning Of Hypocrisy

What Does Hypocrisy Means?

Hypocrisy is the practice of engaging in the same behavior or activity for which one criticizes another or the practice of claiming to have moral standards or beliefs to which one's own behavior does not conform. In moral psychology, it is the failure to follow one's own expressed moral rules and principles. If you accuse a person of being a hypocrite it means that the person pretends to have virtues, moral or religious beliefs, principles, etc., that he or she does not actually possess

In essence, "hypocrisy" refers to the act of claiming to believe something but acting in a different manner. The word is derived from the Greek term for "actor" literally, "one who wears a mask" in other words, someone who pretends to be what he is not.According to British political philosopher David Runciman, "Other kinds of hypocritical deception include claims to knowledge that one lacks, claims to a consistency that one cannot sustain, claims to a loyalty that one does not possess, claims to an identity that one does not hold".

Hypocrisy has been a subject of folk wisdom and wisdom literature from the beginnings of human history. Increasingly, since the 1980s, it has also become central to studies in behavioral economics, cognitive science, cultural psychology, decision making, ethics, evolutionary psychology, moral psychology, political sociology, positive psychology, social psychology, and sociological social psychology.

The Bible calls hypocrisy a sin. There are two forms hypocrisy can take: that of professing belief in something and then acting in a manner contrary to that belief, and that of looking down on others when we ourselves are flawed.

The prophet Isaiah condemned the hypocrisy of his day: "The Lord says, 'These people come near to me with their mouth and honor me with their lips, but their hearts are far from me. Their worship of me is made up only of rules taught by men'" – **(Isaiah 29:13)**. Centuries later, Jesus quoted this verse, aiming the same condemnation at the religious leaders of His day. – **(Matthew 15:8-9)**. John the Baptist refused to give hypocrites a pass, telling them to produce "fruits worthy of repentance" –**(Luke 3:8)**. Jesus took an equally staunch stand against sanctimony, He called hypocrites "wolves in sheep's clothing" **(Matthew 7:15)**, "whitewashed tombs" **(Matthew 23:27)**, "snakes," and "brood of vipers" **(Matthew 23:33)**.

We cannot say we love God if we do not love our brothers **(1 John 2:9)**. Love must be "without hypocrisy" **(Romans 12:9, NKJV)**. A hypocrite may look righteous on the outside, but it is a façade. True righteousness comes from the inner transformation of the Holy Spirit not an external conformity to a set of rules **(Matthew 23:5; 2 Corinthians 3:8)**.

Jesus addressed the other form of hypocrisy in the Sermon on the Mount: "Why do you look at the speck of sawdust in your brother's eye and pay no attention to the plank in your own eye? How can you say to your brother, 'Let me take the speck out of your eye,' when all the time there is a plank in your own eye? You hypocrite, first take the plank out of your own eye, and then you will see clearly to remove the speck from your brother's eye" **(Matthew 7:3-5).** Jesus is not teaching against discernment or helping others overcome sin; instead, He is telling us not be so prideful and convinced of our own goodness that we criticize others from a position of self-righteousness. We should do some introspection first and correct our own shortcomings before we go after the "specks" in others **(cf. Romans 2:1).**

During Jesus' earthly ministry, He had many run-ins with the religious leaders of the day, the Pharisees. These men were well versed in the Scriptures and zealous about following every letter of the Law **(Acts 26:5).** However, in adhering to the letter of the Law, they actively sought loopholes that allowed them to violate the spirit of the Law. Also, they displayed a lack of compassion toward their fellow man and were often overly demonstrative of their so-called spirituality in order to garner praise **(Matthew 23:5–7; Luke 18:11).** Jesus denounced their behavior in no uncertain terms, pointing out that "justice, mercy, and faithfulness" are more important than pursuing a perfection based on faulty standards **(Matthew 23:23).** Jesus made it clear that the problem was not with the Law but the way in which the Pharisees implemented it **(Matthew 23:2-3).** Today, the word pharisee has become synonymous with hypocrite.

It must be noted that hypocrisy is not the same as taking a stand against sin. For example, it is not hypocrisy to teach that drunkenness is a sin, unless the one teaching against drunkenness gets drunk every weekend that would be hypocrisy.

As children of God, we are called to strive for holiness **(1 Peter 1:16).** We are to "hate what is evil" and "cling to what is good" **(Romans 12:9).** We should never imply an acceptance of sin, especially in our own lives. All we do should be consistent with what we believe and who we are in Christ. Play-acting is meant for the stage, not for real life.

Hypocrisy is not a common word in the Old Testament, but the New Testament is rife with examples. This isn't surprising since the word itself comes from the Greek stage acting. It came to mean "acting a part." Advertising something on the outside that is not consistent with the character on the inside is the picture of hypocrisy. When an actor puts on a mask and pretends to be someone he is not, his appearance is different than who he is behind the mask. When this happens morally, it is called hypocrisy.

Though the word itself doesn't appear there, **Mark 11:12-25** gives a vivid picture of hypocrisy. Here, on the heels of Palm Sunday, Jesus curses a fig tree. It seems an odd action given the context. But it is an enacted parable. The fig tree is an illustration of the temple. The fig tree advertises having fruit and being ready for nourishing a passerby but it's deceptive. The fig tree is being a hypocrite. Outwardly beautiful, inwardly rotten or empty. This is why Mark sandwiches the cleansing of the temple between the discussion of the fig tree. The fig tree is a picture of the temple and its religious leaders/system.

The opposite of a hypocrite is to be sincere. It is to be authentic to be pure and unpolluted. It is to be the same on the inside as you are projecting on the outside. **(Philippians 1:10)** gives us an example of this word. This can be illustrated by the ancient world of pottery. Dishonest pottery salesmen would fill in cracks with hard pearly wax these cracks couldn't be detected unless you put them up to the sun. But once held up to the sun, the crack would become evident. So a vase would be "sun-judged" if it passed the test, then it would be considered "without wax" or sine-cera. This is where our word sincere comes from. It means to be pure with integrity and not having hidden cracks. You are on the inside what you advertise on the outside.

Is Hypocrisy A Sin?

Ask Ananias and Sapphira if God classifies hypocrisy as a sin. In Acts 4 we see that these religious leaders lied about what they had given, and they were struck dead. It's a shocking story in the New Testament, but it's an indicator of how serious God takes hypocrisy. This and Jesus' narrative of cursing the fig tree shows how God views this particular sin.

Why Is Hypocrisy Such A Big Deal?

Hypocrisy is a big deal because we are image-bearers. Each human is supposed to be a representative of who God is. It has been said that "our lives either tell the truth about God or they tell a lie." The story of the Bible is that we are image-bearers, but that image has been shattered through our sin. This means that we all tell some lies about God's character. But there is a special type of hypocrisy for those who promote and present themselves as representatives of God (is this not what it means to be a Christian? A "little Christ"?) This is why it is so odious. When we say one thing with our lips but do another with our lifestyle, we are misrepresenting God.

The Deadly Sin of Hypocrisy (Acts 4:36-5:11)

A 12-year-old boy was waiting for his first orthodontist appointment and was a bit nervous. Apparently he wanted to impress the dentist. On the patient questionnaire, in the space marked "Hobbies," he had written, "Swimming and flossing" (Reader's Digest [8/94], p. 112).

That's a humorous example of how we're all prone to hypocrisy. But spiritual hypocrisy is not humorous; it's a dangerous and deadly sin. The hypocrisy of professing Christians has served as an excuse for many to disregard the claims of Christ, saying, "The church is full of hypocrites." The hypocrisy of Christian leaders has caused many believers to stumble. While Jesus was tender with many notorious sinners, He used scathing language to denounce those guilty of religious hypocrisy.

The story of Ananias and Sapphira warns us of the danger of the sin of hypocrisy. It was literally deadly for this couple. Someone has said that if God dealt with all hypocrites in the church as He dealt with this couple, our churches would become morgues!

We are not told whether or not Ananias and Sapphira were true believers in Jesus Christ. Some argue that they were; some that they were not. Perhaps we are not told because if we knew that they were not true Christians, we would shrug their story off as not applying to us. If we knew that they were true Christians, we might say, "Thank God that this was just a one-time occurrence!" We would not pause and ask ourselves, "Is my faith in Christ genuine? Do I need to deal with the sin of hypocrisy?" We do know that Ananias and Sapphira were a part of the early church. Their story applies to us all!

In Acts 4, we saw the enemy attacking the church from without. The Jewish leaders persecuted the apostles and threatened them with more severe measures if they continued to preach in the name of Jesus. But in spite of (or perhaps because of) their threats, the church continued to grow dramatically. There was a spirit of unity, love, and unusual generosity among the believers **(4:32-35).** In this context, we are given a positive example of a godly man, Joseph, better known as Barnabas **(4:36-37).** Then we are given the example of this couple, who put on the mask of hypocrisy and were struck dead by God **(5:1-11).** This threat of seduction from within is much more subtle and dangerous than opposition from without. It is especially a danger when a church is experiencing God's blessing and power.

The lesson is:

Because we are all prone to the deadly sin of hypocrisy, we should diligently pursue godly character.

1. We are all prone to the deadly sin of hypocrisy.

We need to be clear on the exact nature of the sin of Ananias and Sapphira. Their sin was not that they had sold their property and had given only a part to the church. In fact, Peter makes plain (5:4) that it would not have been a sin for them to have sold their property and not given anything to the church. Their sin was that they conspired together to deceive the apostles and the church into thinking that they were giving the entire amount, when in fact they kept back a portion for themselves. In other words, they were trying to impress everyone with a higher level of spirituality and commitment than they really had.

Have you ever done that? I hope you do not say "no," or we might need to have a sudden funeral this day! We've all been guilty of trying to impress others with our commitment and devotion to Christ, even though we know in our heart that we are exaggerating. A pastor had been preaching on the importance of daily Bible reading. He and his wife were invited over to a parishioner's home for dinner. His wife saw a note on the kitchen calendar: "Pastor/Mrs. for dinner—Dust all Bibles" (Reader's Digest [3/90], p. 129).

Note four things about hypocrisy:

The Seriousness Of Hypocrisy:

Liberal commentators are shocked at this sudden, severe punishment. Ananias is not given a chance to repent, even though his sin seems not all that serious. His wife is not even told of her husband's death and of what will happen to her if she lies. The instant that she agrees with her husband's lie, she is struck dead. In this age of tolerance, we might think, "What's the big deal?"

But we need to view this sin from God's holy perspective, not from our world's relativistic view. Jesus always hit hypocrisy hard. In

Matthew 23, He pronounced many woes on the scribes and Pharisees, whom He repeatedly called hypocrites. He warned His disciples, "Beware of the leaven of the Pharisees, which is hypocrisy" **(Luke 12:1).** Like leaven, hypocrisy starts small and unnoticed. It doesn't seem to be a big deal. But if it is not quickly checked, it spreads. It deceives the person into thinking that things are right between him and God, when in reality, things are very wrong.

The leaven of hypocrisy can soon infect an entire church. The church at Laodicea thought that things were going well. They said, "I am rich, and have become wealthy, and have need of nothing." But the Lord's perspective was, "You do not know that you are wretched and miserable and poor and blind and naked" **(Rev. 3:17)!**

Some ask why God dealt with Ananias and Sapphira so severely when He does not do so with other hypocrites in the church. Probably, it was because the church was in its infancy, and He needed to set before us a sober lesson of the seriousness of this sin among God's people. He did the same thing with Achan **(Joshua 7; see**

also Lev. 10:1-3; 2 Sam. 6:6-7). The word "church" first occurs in Acts in verse 11 (out of 16 times). The word means an assembly or congregation of people. Luke wants us to know that the church should live in the holy fear of God and especially should be on guard against this serious sin, hypocrisy.

The Subjects Of Hypocrisy:

This couple that fell into this sin were professing Christians, "members" of the church in Jerusalem. This means that we're all in danger of falling into this subtle sin. We don't want other Christians or those outside the church to think that we have problems. That wouldn't be a good testimony, would it? So we put on our spiritual mask when we're around others, even though we know and our family knows that we do not live as we profess to live. When a prominent Christian is shown to be a hypocrite, the world heaves a sigh of relief, thinking, "Christians are really no different than anyone else. If they're phonies, then Christianity must not be true."

Notice also that this sin affects both men and women. Some sins may be more prevalent in men, while other sins are more prevalent with women. But both sexes are vulnerable to hypocrisy. Ananias and Sapphira had agreed together to this act of deception (5:9). Whether you are male or female, you need to guard yourself against hypocrisy.

By the way, some argue that a wife should submit to her husband, even if he asks her to join him in doing wrong. This story shows the error of that view. When Peter asked Sapphira whether they sold the land for the amount that her husband had claimed, she should have obeyed God above her husband (5:29) by telling the truth.

The Selfishness Of Hypocrisy:

Motive is everything in this sin. If Ananias and Sapphira had sold their land and had told the apostles, "We feel led to give half to the church," it would not have been a problem. Their sin was the evil intent of their hearts, to make others think that they were more spiritual than they really were. They were motivated by love of self, not by love of God and others.

God, who always knows the motives of our hearts, judged them on the spot.

Hypocrisy is always motivated by self-love. We want to impress others, to make them think that we are something that we know in our hearts we are not. Kids, by the way, have a built-in antenna to detect hypocrisy in their parents. Nothing turns kids away from the faith as quickly as hypocritical parents. If they hear you put on your spiritual voice around church people, but you verbally abuse them at home, they can see right through you. They will not be drawn to follow the God you profess to follow. That's why it is crucial for parents to acknowledge their wrongs and ask forgiveness of their children when they sin against them.

The Short-Sightedness Of Hypocrisy:

Hypocrisy is short-sighted in several ways:

a.) Hypocrisy Focuses On Group Dynamics, Not On Personal Reality With God.
It was an exciting thing to be in the Jerusalem church in those days. There were the large

gatherings in Solomon's portico, where
thousands heard the apostles preach about Jesus
(5:12; 2:47). The church had an unusual sense
of unity and caring (4:32). The apostles were
performing extraordinary miracles to confirm
the message of the gospel (4:33; 5:16). Every
day there were stories of more people getting
saved (5:14). Even by those on the outside held
the church in high esteem (5:13). It was easy to
get caught up in the group dynamic and to ride
on the bandwagon of what was happening, but
to lack personal reality with God. That's what
happened to Ananias and Sapphira.

It's always exciting to be a part of a movement
of God's Holy Spirit. Some of us were a part of
the Jesus movement of the 1970's. The church I
grew up in couldn't attract more than a handful
for a midweek service! But I used to go out for
choir ministerations and thousands of young
people would be there for a mid-week service.
The singing was not the traditional hymns, sung
halfheartedly to the accompaniment of the
organ and piano. Everyone enthusiastically sang
new praise choruses, accompanied by
musicians playing guitars and drums. It was a
great experience to join in with that sort of

gathering. And yet, while many young people truly got saved, there were always some that were just riding on the group experience. It was always sad when they would later fall into some serious sin and abandon the faith.

One of the main ways to avoid hypocrisy is to make sure that you are walking in reality with God every day. Have you personally trusted in Christ as your Savior and Lord? Do you spend time in His Word and in prayer on a regular basis? Do you deal with the sin in your life, especially on the heart level, when His Word confronts you with where you are wrong? If not, you have to start faking it when you're around other Christians, to keep up the appearance that you're doing fine. That's the beginning of hypocrisy.

Ray Stedman (transcribed message, "Body Life," Peninsula Bible Church, 4/26/70) pointed out that the moment we start pretending to be what we really are not, death enters in, because we are cut off from the vital reality of communion with Christ and His body, the church. We lose the reality of walking in the

Spirit. To avoid hypocrisy, we must maintain daily reality with the Lord.

b.) Hypocrisy Does Not Focus On What God Thinks, But On What People Thinks.
Ananias and Sapphira wanted to look good in front of the apostles and the rest of the church. Barnabas had just given the total amount of a sale of some property. Everyone thought highly of Barnabas. Ananias and Sapphira wanted everyone to think highly of them. But, sadly, they didn't stop to consider what the living God thought about them.

To avoid hypocrisy, you must live daily with the aim of pleasing God above all else. The minute you start trying to look good to others, without being concerned about what God thinks, you are into hypocrisy. Both Peter and Barnabas later fell into this sin. The church in Antioch had both Jews and Gentiles together in one fellowship. When Peter first visited there, he ate together with the Gentiles, contrary to Jewish customs. But when the Jewish circumcision party showed up, Peter withdrew and only ate with the Jews, out of fear for what they would think. Peter's hypocrisy wrongly influenced Barnabas. Paul confronted him publicly, and to his credit, Peter accepted the rebuke **(Gal. 2:11-14).** If such godly men as Peter and Barnabas could be carried away by this sin, then certainly we all need to be on guard!

c.) Hypocrisy Focuses On This Life, Not On Eternity.
If Ananias and Sapphira had been thinking about the shortness of life and the certainty of judgment and eternity, they would not have done what they did. But whether we get struck down instantly for our sin or have to stand before God at the judgment, in a few short years we all will face God. Scripture reminds us, "Nothing in all creation is hidden from God's sight. Everything is uncovered and laid bare before the eyes of him to whom we must give account" **(Heb. 4:13, NIV).** Twice our text mentions that great fear came on all those who heard of what happened to Ananias and Sapphira (5:6, 11). Great fear of God should come on us as well! We're all a heartbeat away from standing before God and giving an account. Keeping eternity in view will keep us from the sin of hypocrisy.

Ananias and Sapphira warn us of the deadly sin of hypocrisy. But our text not only warns us about what not to be; it also shows us, in both Barnabas and Peter, how we should live.

2. We should diligently pursue godly character.

These men show us four aspects of godly character:

a. To Pursue Godly Character, We Must Grow In The Fulness Of The Holy Spirit And Of Faith.
We have already seen (2:4) how the apostles were all filled with the Holy Spirit. Again, before he preached before the council, Peter was filled with the Spirit (4:8). In 11:24 we read that Barnabas "was a good man, full of the Holy Spirit and of faith." It was the Holy Spirit who showed Peter that Ananias was being deceptive. Peter accuses him of lying to the Holy Spirit (5:3), whom Peter also calls God (5:4).

By way of contrast, Peter says that Satan had filled Ananias' heart (5:3). As we have seen, to be filled means to be controlled. Peter and Barnabas were under the control of the Holy Spirit, the third person of the Trinity. Ananias and Sapphira were controlled by Satan in their act of deception because they had yielded to his temptation. Being full of the Holy Spirit and of faith does not mean that a believer will be sinless. As we have seen, both Peter and Barnabas later fell into hypocrisy themselves. But it does mean a daily walk of dependence on the Spirit, yielding to Him so that the fruit of the Spirit grows in our lives. To be full of faith means that we daily trust in God and His promises, rather than leaning on our own schemes or on worldly wisdom.

b. To Pursue Godly Character, We Must Grow In The Ministry Of Encouragement.
We hardly remember Barnabas' real name, Joseph, because his nickname is so prominent. Scholars cannot determine the etymology of the name, but Luke translates it for us as meaning, "son of encouragement." "Son of" was a common Hebrew designation for a dominating characteristic. James and John were "sons of thunder." Judas was the "son of perdition."

Barnabas was so marked by his encouraging spirit that he was the "son of encouragement."

You communicate encouragement by your attitude, your actions, and your words. An encouraging person has an attitude of trust and hope in God that makes others look to His promises. He acts in ways that encourage those who are down. This may mean helping a person with some overwhelming task, or just taking the time to listen to the person's problems. His words are not sarcastic and demeaning, but full of hope and love. He communicates, "I believe that in the Lord's strength, you will live in a manner pleasing to Him." All of us should seek to be sons of encouragement.

c . TO Pursue Godly Character, We Musr Grow In The Ministry Of Generosity.
Barnabas sold a piece of property and gave it all to the apostles to use in meeting the needs of the poor among them. Barnabas was of priestly descent, and according to the Law, priests could not own property (Num. 18:20; Deut. 10:9). Whether this law was no longer observed (after the exile) or whether Barnabas had just inherited some land and was disposing of it, we

do not know. But we do know that he could have spent the money on himself, but he chose to give it to the Lord's work. As I emphasized last week, believers will grow to be like Jesus, who was rich, but for our sakes became poor, that we, through His poverty might be rich (2 Cor. 8:9). No doubt greed was a factor that motivated Ananias and Sapphira to hold back part of the profit from the sale of their land. As believers, we must put all greed to death and grow in generosity by sharing what God has given to us.

d. To Pursue Godly Character, We Must Grow In Integrity.
I imagine that Ananias and Sapphira's gift was quite substantial. If Peter had not been a man of integrity, he could have thought, "I dare not offend these wealthy donors." Even if he suspected some deception, he would have been careful to praise them for their generosity in hopes that they would give more in the future. But Peter was more concerned with purity in the church than he was with taking a gift that was given with the wrong motives. So he strongly confronted their deception.

Liberal commentators castigate Peter because, they say, he did not display the grace that Jesus showed toward sinners. They say that he was more of the spirit of Elijah calling down fire from heaven, than of Jesus who offered forgiveness to sinners. But Peter did not pronounce the death sentence on Ananias. He rebuked him, but I believe that Peter was a bit surprised when Ananias dropped dead in front of him. With Sapphira, he predicted that the same thing that had just happened to her husband would happen to her. But Peter was simply God's instrument to speak His truth. It was God who cleansed His church of these hypocrites.

Any time we take a strong stand against sin in the church, someone will accuse us of not being loving. But to tolerate sin in the church, sin that will spread like leaven and contaminate and destroy many others, is not to act with love or compassion. We must always offer forgiveness and restoration to those who repent. But we must never tolerate sin under the banner of love. People of integrity hold both to kindness and truth (Prov. 3:3).

Are Christians Hypocrites?

Yes. But we shouldn't be. The only One who was never hypocritical is the Lord Jesus. He was always consistent inside and outside. We should be people of sincerity. The truth, though, is that believers are being changed into the image of Christ. Though many have given Christianity a bad name, there are many sincere and authentic believers in Jesus. One of these dear saints was John Newton. Newton spoke well of sincerity and simplicity. He notes that this grace can only come through the gospel. We are by nature hypocrites, only through growth in the gospel will we see hypocrisy rooted out. Here is Newton in his own words:

"The true simplicity, which is the honor and strength of a believer, is the effect of a spiritual perception of the truths of the Gospel. It arises from, and bears a proportion to, the sense we have of our own unworthiness, the power and grace of Christ, and the greatness of our obligations to him. So far as our knowledge of these things is vital and experimental, it will make us simple-hearted. This simplicity may be considered in two respects, a simplicity of intention, and a simplicity of dependence. The former stands in opposition to the corrupt workings of self, the latter to the false reasoning of unbelief."

Chapter Two

The Signs Of Hypocrisy

A Christian is one who has faith in Jesus Christ being their savior (Eph 1:12-13). Faith is possessing the belief that Christ died on the cross for the forgiveness of all our sins (1 Cor 15:3), was buried and rose again (1 Cor 15:4), so that we may have everlasting life (Rom 6:22, 1 Cor 15:22). The requirement for salvation today is much easier than in times past (2 Cor 11:3, Rom 3:21)! Although we may see results from a believer's life, we cannot know for certain that they possess the faith required for salvation. Believers today are members of the church the body of Christ (Col 1:24). God now sees us in Christ, and not who we see when we look in the mirror!

We are not righteous enough for God on our own merits (Titus 3:5). The good news is that our belief in what Jesus Christ did on our behalf makes us the righteousness of God (1 Cor 1:30, 2 Cor 5:21)! Christ's death was sufficient to

God for the forgiveness of our sins (2 Cor 5:19, 2 Cor 5:21, Rom 6:22), and Christ's resurrection was for our justification (Rom 4:25).

The sin barrier between God and man was removed through Christ's crucifixion (Rom 6:22, 2 Cor 5:21). God can now work through us once we've removed ourselves from His path (Col 2:14, Philippians 1:6). We can focus on what we can do for Him once we've stopped focusing on ourselves and our iniquities (Rom 7:22-25). Basically, we don't work in order to be saved, we work because we are saved (Eph 2:10, Eph 4:12), and it is our works that will be judged at the judgement seat of Christ, not we ourselves as believers (1 Cor 3:15). Works, with the belief that it is to obtain or maintain salvation, actually puts us in debt with God as this shows lack of faith in Christ (Rom 4:4, Eph 2:8-9). If you're asking for forgiveness of sins for example, who's doing the asking? We can't save ourselves (Titus 3:5), which is why we need faith in Christ (2 Cor 1:9). Forgiveness occurred when Christ died on the cross regardless of our belief (2 Cor 5:19). Salvation occurs at the moment of belief (Eph 1:13).

It is of utmost importance to rightly divide the word of truth (2 Tim 2:15), the gospel of our salvation (Eph 1:13) that was given to our Apostle Paul, from that of biblical Israel when studying the bible. Jesus, while living, and the 12 apostles were for the lost sheep of the house of Israel, which was not you or I (Mat 10:5-6, Mat 15:24). Paul received the revelation of the fellowship of the mystery from Christ resurrected (Eph 3:9), which was before kept secret since the beginning of time (Rom 16:25). Had this mystery information been known prior to Christ's death, the princes of this world would not have crucified Jesus (1 Cor 2:8).

We today are no longer under the law of Moses (Rom 6:14), but under God's dispensation of grace (Eph 3:2). We must simply have faith in Christ's finished cross work as payment for our sins (Rom 3:28, 1 Cor 15:3, Gal 2:20, Col 2:13, 2 Cor 5:19), and that Christ was buried and rose again for our justification (2 Cor 1:9, Rom 4:25). It is the gift of God made possible by His grace (Rom 5:18), and our belief is acceptance of His free gift (Eph 2:8. Eph 1:13). You'll find doctrine for how we are to live today in the 13

epistles of Paul, Romans through Philemon
(Rom 3:21).

When you're a passenger in a vehicle, you have
faith that the driver will safely get you to your
destination. Jesus Christ is our 'spiritual driver'
(Rom 5:10, Rom 8:32), and the holy Spirit, our
'spiritual seat-belt' (Eph 4:30), that seals our
souls until the day of redemption at the moment
of belief (Eph 1:13)! We can't lose our
salvation, but living as we should as Christians
can still be difficult at times (Rom 7:23). We
will certainly fail on occasion while Satan
reigns in this present evil world (Gal 1:4, 2 Cor
4:4, Rom 7:24-25), but our resolve should never
waver (2 Cor 7:1), as God's love for us
becomes more evident in our daily walk (2 Cor
13:14).

Since salvation is by faith alone, it is impossible
to tell a true believer from an unbeliever.

Romans 4:5. But to him that worketh not, but
believeth on Him who justifiieth the ungodly,
his faith is counted for righteousness.

Romans 11:6 Salvation is all grace apart from works.

Romans 6:23 For the penalty of sin is death, but the gift of God is eternal life, through Jesus Christ our Lord.

Those who have accepted the free gift of eternal life are saved.

John 3:18 Believers are no longer condemned, but unbelievers are condemned already because they have not believed on the name of the Son of God.

Believers and unbelievers look alike. God knows his sheep but we have no way of knowing except by what people say.

If a person says they believe Jesus died for all their sins and they know they are going to heaven because of what Jesus did for them plus nothing. We have to assume they are saved.

But there are believers who have lost their faith, or do not remember ever believing the gospel. Second Timothy 2:13. If we believe not, after we have once believed, He abideth faithful, He cannot deny Himself.

So there is no outward evidence that a person is saved or lost.

There are many wonderful people in the eyes of the world who may dedicate their lives to a god, but never accept Jesus as their savior.

John 3:18 is the dividing verse in the bible. Knowing who they are may be hard to tell. You cannot tell a book by its cover and you cannot tell who has believed the gospel and is saved except by what they say.

Romans 8:9 Without the spirit of God their is no salvation. With the spirit we have eternal life. Ephesians 1:13-14. Guaranteed eternal life of the believer.

God knows His sheep. Second Timothy 2:19 Nevertheless, the foundation of God is sure, having this seal, (Ephesians 1:13) the Lord knoweth them that are His. John 6:39. He has never lost one sheep.

First John 2:2 Jesus died for every sin of everyone in the whole world.

Romans 3:26-28 For He is the just and the justifier of them that believe in Jesus. Since salvation is a free gift from God to all who have believed on Him alone, for the free gift have eternal life.

We have nothing to boast in. Unbelievers may boast in what they do or do not do. But believers have nothing to boast in. Jesus paid it all and we paid 0. You cannot boast in 0.

Romans 1:16. For I am not ashamed of the gospel of Christ, for it is the power of God unto salvation to everyone that "BELIEVETH", to the Jew first, and also to the Greek. Jesus said He will separate them at harvest time. The wheat from the tares.

First John 5:13 These things have I written unto you that BELIEVE on the name of the Son of God, that ye may KNOW YE HAVE ETERNAL LIFE.

How Then Can We Differentiate The Hypocrite's From The True Believers

Sign One;

Hypocrites Pretend To Be Someone They Are Not

The word hypocrite came from the Greek word hupokrites, meaning an "actor under an assumed character" (Strong's Dictionary). A hypocrite uses a mask to hide his true identity and be perceived by others in a way that he is not.

Hypocrites take the pain and effort to look sanctimonious, divine, and sinless. They want people to believe that they are more righteous than others.

Jesus Christ has this to say to hypocrites:

"Woe to you, scribes and Pharisees, hypocrites! For you cleanse the outside of the cup and dish, but inside they are full of extortion and self-indulgence. Blind Pharisee, first cleanse the inside of the cup and dish, that the outside of them may be clean also."

"Woe to you, scribes and Pharisees, hypocrites! For you are like whitewashed tombs which indeed appear beautiful outwardly, but inside are full of dead men's bones and all uncleanness. Even so you also outwardly appear righteous to men, but inside you are full of hypocrisy and lawlessness **(Matthew 23:25-28)."**

"Strong words from the mouth of our Messiah". Hypocrites are public saints but private sinners. Though they look divine, godly character is far from their hearts.

(Job 8:13) tells us:

"… The hope of the hypocrite shall perish." Though the hypocrites may triumph for a little while, they will ultimately be discovered. They can only do so much to hide their true character. Soon enough, people will know the truth and they will be known by their fruits **(Matthew 7:16).**

Sign 2;

Hypocrites Love The Praise Of Men

So, why does a hypocrite puts a great effort to look righteous? Because a hypocrite highly values the praise of men.
Matthew 6:1-2 tells us:
"Take heed that you do not do your charitable deeds before men, to be seen by them. Otherwise, you have no reward from your Father in heaven. Therefore, when you do a charitable deed, do not sound a trumpet before you as the hypocrites do in the synagogues and in the streets,"
That They May Have Glory From Men. Assuredly, I say to you, they have their reward."
You see, hypocrites are after the fame and glory this world could offer. For them, it is the praise and recognition of men that give them value and honor.
Jesus Christ further illustrates how hypocrites love the praise of men. He continues:
"And when you pray, you shall not be like the hypocrites. For they love to pray standing in the synagogues and on the corners of the streets,
That They May Be Seen By Men. Assuredly, I

say to you, they have their reward **(Matthew 6:5).**"
Hypocrites love to pray and what's their main purpose? Is it to draw closer to God? No. They pray for hours and hours so that people may see them pray and cause them to think that they are pious and holy people.
Matthew 23:14 adds that hypocrites love to pray long prayers for a show.
Another example how hypocrites attract attention to themselves is through fasting.

"Moreover, when you fast, do not be like the hypocrites, with a sad countenance. For they disfigure their faces That They May Appear To Men To Be Fasting. Assuredly, I say to you, they have their reward" **(Matthew 6:16).**
Yes, hypocrites may succeed in impressing people and getting their praise, but sadly, as Jesus Christ repeatedly mentioned, they have their reward. Instead of obtaining an everlasting reward from God, they settled for the "Temporary" applause of people.
If what motivates you to do good is to obtain people's attention and praise, then you are a hypocrite. If you only work when your boss is around, if you are just a Christian during church

services, if you give something just tlo impress people, then I'm sorry to say this but you are a hypocrite.
Plain and simple.

Sign 3:

A Hypocrite Is More Concerned Onn Correcting Others Than Themselves

Another sign of being a hypocrite is that they avidly point out the mistakes of others while ignoring theirs. For a hypocrite, they see themselves as righteous and see others as sinners. Thus, they take it to themselves to correct others.While hypocrites may be right in identifying sin when they see one, they must first correct themselves before they can correct others.
We read in **Matthew 7:3-5:**
"And why do you look at the speck in your brother's eye, but do not consider the plank in your own eye? Or how can you say to your brother, 'Let me remove the speck from your eye'; and look, a plank is in your own eye? HYPOCRITE! First remove the plank from

your own eye, and then you will see clearly to remove the speck from your brother's eye."
Jesus Christ is telling us here that a hypocrite is quick in pointing out the sins of others while he is suffering from a bigger and more serious sin. As what was popularly mentioned, "Practice what you preach." You can't expect people to believe you when your life is filled with sin as well.It was also said, "I rather see a sermon than hear one."
So, be careful at judging others when you don't even take the effort of correcting yourself.

Sign 4;

A Hypocrites Puts More Importance In Man-made Tradition.

In one instance, the scribes and Pharisees were furious to see how Jesus openly violate their tradition. They asked Christ:
"Why do Your disciples transgress the tradition of the elders? For they do not wash their hands when they eat bread" **(Matthew 15:2).**

Christ explained to them how they put so much importance on their human tradition that in the process, they violate God's commandment of honoring their father and mother.

Christ further said:

"You have made the commandment of God of no effect by your tradition" (verse 6).

Because of a hypocrite's willingness to look holy to other people, he will desperately think of different ways on how to achieve this. Thus, these hypocrites create man-made traditions to create more opportunities to look pious.

Isn't this strategy all too familiar today? Let me give you an example. In some countries, there are hundreds of fiestas dedicated to different saints. They say it is a time to honor so-called saints, but in reality, they take this as an opportunity to get drunk, stay up late, and play loud music until the rooster crows!

After going to the church, they would spend the rest of the day in festivities and in most cases, forgetting what they just heard from the preacher.

Sad, but true.

Sign no. 5:

A Hypocrite's Heart Is Far From God

Jesus continued His discourse with the scribes and Pharisees by quoting Isaiah.
We read in **Matthew 15:8-9:**
Hypocrites! Well did Isaiah prophesy about you, saying:
'These people draw near to Me with their mouth,
And honor Me with their lips,
But their heart is far from Me.
And in vain they worship Me,
Teaching as doctrines the commandment of men.' "
Hypocrites have mastered the art of lip-service.They know how to fake it through their words. On the surface, through their flowery and religious words, they seem to be praising God.
But God isn't interested in what they are saying, but rather God is more interested in the substance of their hearts.
In the same manner, we can go to church services, sing hymns and praise to God, and

listen to sermons but if our hearts aren't right
with God, we are simply being hypocritical.
Jesus further cemented His statement on how
hypocrites simply value more their traditions
rather than keeping God's commandments.
They are experts in "teaching as doctrines the
commandments of men."
Hypocrites believe that they can be more
righteous than God.
They disregard God's commandments and
replace it with their own invention. This is a
sign of their hearts being far from God even if
they spend so much time worshiping God,
praying, and fasting.

Sign 6;

A Hypocrite Forgets About The Weightier Matter Of The Law

Hypocrites got their focus on the wrong things.
They think much of themselves to the point that
they forget what truly matters.
We read in **(Matthew 23:24)**
"Woe to you, scribes and Pharisees, hypocrites!
For you pay tithe of mint and anise and
cummin, and have neglected the weightier

matters of the law: "Justice And Mercy And Faith". These you ought to have done, without leaving the others undone. Blind guides, who strain out a gnat and swallow a camel!"
The scribes and Pharisees are highly meticulous in paying their tithes. They make sure that they have all the calculations right. Even the smallest grain, they still count and put every effort to never overlook anything.
Now, there's nothing wrong in doing your best in following the law. As a matter of fact, Jesus Christ even said that these are things they ought to do meaning, they should give their tithes.

There's nothing wrong with the law. If there's something wrong here, it was their attitude. They were strict, precise, and meticulous in following the less significant matter of the law while they are careless in observing the WEIGHTIER matters of the law.
What are these? They are justice, mercy, and faith.
They neglected being just to their neighbor.
They forgot to be merciful to others.
And most certainly, they put more faith in themselves than God.

Jesus went on to say that these hypocrites are blind guides who strain out a gnat and swallow a camel! The hypocrites will warn others of every small violation of the law but will not bother correcting them or their selves when it comes to sins with bigger consequences.

They were so strict that keeping the commandments and laws of God has been a burden!

(I John 5:3) tells us:

"For this is the love of God, that we keep His commandments. And His commandments are not burdensome."

Now, don't get me wrong. It is never the intention of Jesus here that we don't take "little" sins seriously. In fact, He is telling us to beware of both the lesser and weightier matters of the law. We can't simply be too concerned about little sins and at the same time, forget about the bigger sins. That would be hypocrisy. We must be about overcoming every sin in our lives, be it small or big. In doing so, we can avoid becoming a hypocrite.

Sign no. 7:

A Hypocrite Is Self-Righteous

If it is difficult to identify hypocrisy, wait until
you mixed it up with self-righteousness.
The combination of hypocrisy and self-
righteousness is FATAL. It can easily make a
Christian spiritually blind and terminally
deceived.

Matthew 23:29-30 tells us:
"Woe to you, scribes and Pharisees, hypocrites!
Because you build the tombs of the prophets
and adorn the monuments of the righteous, and
say, 'If we had lived in the days of our fathers,
we would not have been partakers with them in
the blood of the prophets.'"
As you can see here, a hypocrite seems to be
serving other people but it was never from the
heart. They can put up a show of good deeds
and yet, they don't actually want to do it. In
truth, they are just forced to do so to please
other people.
Here is where hypocrisy meets self-
righteousness. Jesus explained that while they
are honoring the memory of the prophets, in
their heart, they are speaking of how righteous
they are.

The hypocrite believes that if they were alive during the time of the prophets, they would not have joined those people who have killed them! For the scribes and Pharisees, they believe that they will "never" fall into the same trap of persecuting the prophets. But here they are persecuting the greatest prophet of all time Jesus Christ!

Because of their self-righteousness, they can't see that in fact, they are committing the same mistakes that their forefathers committed. These hypocrites think that they are better than their ancestors, but in fact, they are doing the same thing with Christ.A self-righteous hypocrite would think of themselves as more spiritually superior than others. They are quick to find faults in others while ignoring their own sins.

Sign 8;

A Hypocrite May Be Influenced By The Gospel In Every Part Of Himself.

He may come to great knowledge of God's truth **(Heb 6:4).** His emotions about Christ may be high **(Matt 13:20).** He may even experience drastic changes in the outward man, like the Pharisee who prayed, "God, I thank You that I am not as other men are, extortioners, unjust, adulterers, etc." **(Lk 18:11–12).**

Sign 9;

A Hypocrite May Look To Others Like He's A True Believer.

He might talk of the law and the gospel **(Ps 50:16),** openly confess his sin to his own shame **(1 Sam 26:21),** and humble himself in sackcloth **(1 Kgs 21:27).** He may even carefully consider what duties he needs to perform and seek after them **(Is 58:2),** persevere even in hard times, give his possessions away to God and the saints, or even give his body away to be burned **(1 Cor 13:3).**

Sign 10;

A hypocrite may advance far in God's ordinary graces.

He may come under great convictions of sin, just as Judas did **(Matt 27:3–5).** He may tremble at the word of God, just as Felix did **(Acts 24:25),** rejoice in receiving the truth **(Matt 13:20),** and have many experiences of tasting the good graces of God **(Heb 6:4).**

Sign 11;

A Hypocrite May Have Some Characteristics Very Similar To The Saving Graces Of The Holy Spirit.

He may have a kind of faith, like Simon Magus who "believed also" **(Acts 8:13)** but then proved to be a false believer. He may have a kind of legal and outward repentance that looks very much like true repentance **(Mal 3:14).** He may have a great and powerful fear of God, like

Balaam did **(Num 22:18).** He may experience a kind of hope **(Job 8:13).** The hypocrite may even have some love, as Herod had of John **(Mk 6:26).**

Sign 12;

A hypocrite can even have great and powerful experiences of God.

He may have "tasted of the heavenly gift" and become "partakers of the Holy Spirit" and experienced the "powers of the age to come" and yet not be genuinely converted.

So, what are the marks of a true believer? How is genuine conversion to be distinguished from false conversion? Guthrie provides five marks of a true believer that are not possessed by the hypocrite.

Signs Of A True Believer

Many people claim to be believers but have no clue what it means to be a true Christian. There are many signs that a person will show if they are a true believer in Christ that will differentiate them from unbelievers who are not truly saved yet.

Who Are True Believers?

True believers are simply people who have been truly saved from sin by believing in the Lord Jesus Christ and washed by His blood by accepting Him as their personal Lord and saviour.

This implies that a person who is a true believer is saved and follows the bible teachings of Jesus Christ wholeheartedly

On the other hand, if a person is an unbeliever or not a true believer of Christ Jesus, they won't be saved nor will they have any desire to obey or follow the teachings of Jesus Christ.

Major Signs Of True Believers.

Below are the signs of true believers that everyone who is truly saved and has believed in the Lord Jesus Christ will show.

1. A true believer's heart is changed forever.
In **(Jeremiah 32:39)** the Lord says, "I will give them one heart, and one way, that they may fear me forever." Hypocrites never have a changed

nature. Hypocrites want Christ for the good that He might do them in the world. But a true believer's heart loves Christ as the all-satisfying treasure of this life and the next.

2. A True believer's changed life comes from a heart of love to Christ. Hypocrites can clean up their outward behavior to be seen by men, to ease their troubled consciences, or to keep themselves from the consequences of their sins.

But True believers of Jesus Christ truly and fervently love God with all their hearts, soul, strength and might which is the greatest commandment God has given to mankind.And this fervent love for God in any believer will be evident by the kind of lifestyle they live and the obedience they show to God.
You can't say you love God if you have no interest in obeying in word in the bible which is sadly the case with most so-called Christians which is why Jesus Christ said in **(John 14:15)** that if you truly love Him, you will keep His commandments. Couldn't be simpler than that.

3. A True believer seeks Christ and His kingdom above all else.

This is the one thing necessary: Christ's friendship and fellowship. But that is never the "one thing" and heart-satisfying choice of the hypocrites. True believers, on the other hand, desire that this "better part would never be taken from them" **(Lk 10:42).**

4. A True believer submits to the righteousness of God.
He abandons all hope in himself and his own righteousness, and rests wholly in the righteousness of Christ for his acceptance before God. A true believer rests in Christ and Him only as his Savior. Hypocrites don't do this **(Rom 10:3).** They depend, in some degree, upon their own righteousness.

5. A True believer has the three great essentials of genuine Christianity.
First, he is broken in heart and emptied of his own righteousness so as to loath himself **(Lk 19:10).** Second, he takes up Christ Jesus as the only treasure and jewel that can enrich and satisfy **(Matt 13:44).** Third, he sincerely closes with Christ's whole yoke without exception, judging all His "will just and good, holy and

spiritual" **(Rom 7:12)**. A hypocrite does none of these things.

6. A True believer Practices Forgiveness.
One of the signs of a true believer that will show that someone is a believer in Christ Jesus is that they will practice forgiveness and won't hold grudges against their offenders.
If you claim to be a true Christian, you will easily forgive others who have deeply hurt you in one way or the other even it may be difficult at times but you must remember we live in a fallen world of broken and sinful people.
So, it is inevitable that people will hurt you including the ones close to you but you must forgive anyway because if you don't you also won't be forgiven by your heavenly Father as well **(Matthews 6:14,15)**.

7. A True believer Imitates Christ.
If you are a genuine believer who has been saved by the saving grace of our Lord Jesus Christ, you will imitate Him and not the world or the evil people of this world.**(Ephesians 5:1)** This implies that your lifestyle speaks and reflect the nature of Christ be it in the way you dress, conduct yourself or interact with others.

In short, your life conforms o the image of Jesus Christ as **(2 Corinthians 6:18)** wonderfully puts it.

On the other hand, if you are not a genuine believer in Christ Jesus yet, you won't imitate Him but you will instead imitate your master Satan and his demons because he who sins is of the devil **(1 John 3:8).**

8.A True believer has genuine faith in God. One of the signs that will show you are a true believer in Jesus Christ is that you will have a new faith and this genuine faith will be the living faith based on Jesus Christ alone who can give you eternal life.

There are many religious faiths in this world but not all of them will give you eternal life and save you from the wrath to come as most of these religious faiths are from Satan put there intending to lead many astray from Christ into their eternal perdition in hell.Only real faith in Jesus Christ and His word found in **(Mark 16:16)** can save you from hell and help you make it for heaven when you die and this is the real living faith you will have if you are true believers who have been saved from sin.

9. Obeying Christ **(John 14:15)**

When you become a true believer or true Christian, you will obey the teachings of Jesus Christ found in God's word wholeheartedly and not some of the teachings as some so-called believers do but you will obey Christ fully and not partially.

A person who claims to be a genuine believer will live a Christian life that's in full obedience to Jesus Christ and won't allow their sinful flesh to dictate their lives.But if you are not a genuine believer yet, you won't obey our Lord Jesus Christ. Instead, you will follow your pernicious sinful ways **(2 Peter 2:2)** which will just eventually lead you to eternal destruction in hell.

10. Loves Others Selflessly.

If you are a genuine believer with a definite salvation experience in your life who is truly saved and on your way to heaven, you will be filled with God's love that will enable you to love others selflessly the way Christ expects you to.

It's this true selfless agape love **(1 Corinthians 13:4-8)** talks about that only comes from God and is imparted to you when you accept Christ Jesus into your heart that will enable you to selflessly love others without any selfish motives.

As humans, we are naturally selfish and self-centred which is why we can't truly and selflessly love other people unless they are benefiting us in some way but when you become a genuine believer, this selfish nature will be removed from you are replaced with selfless agape love.

11. Heavenly-Minded.

Being heavenly minded is also one of the major signs of a true believer that a person will manifest if that person is truly saved and a true Christian on their way to heaven.

The apostle Paul in Colossians 3:2 encourages believers to set their affections on heavenly things above where our home is and not on earthly things which will eventually pass away. If you are a true believer, your real affections will be on things above and not of the earth but if you are an unbeliever or a fake believer, you will be earthly-minded which will manifest by the way you live and think.

12. Brings Good Fruits **(Matthew 7:18-20; Galatians 5:22-23).**

A person who is a genuine believer will bring forth good fruits of the Holy Spirit because that person is a good tree with the new nature of Christ in them that enables them to bear good fruits
Jesus Christ said in **(John 15:4-6)**that only if we abide in Him we will be able to bring forth good fruits which will be shown by our good works and good deeds as He's the vine and we as true believers we are the branches.
On the other hand, if you are not a true believer yet, you are a bad tree Jesus Christ talks about in **(Luke 6:43)** that will bring forth all manner of bad fruits and evil deeds as He is not in you yet.

13. Live Godly.
Someone who is a true Christian who has believed and fully accepted our Lord Jesus Christ as their personal Lord and saviour will live godly in this present evil world.

This will be so because of God's grace **(Titus 2:11)** talks about that brings salvation which has appeared to everyone and it's this grace that enables a true believer to deny all forms of ungodliness so that they can live godly and soberly in this present sinful world. Nevertheless, if you are a fake believer who is just religious and goes to church every Sunday, this grace will simply be nowhere to be seen in your life, dear which is why you find living a godly life that's above sin difficult and impossible.

14. New Hunger For Righteousness.
When you become a true believer in Christ after becoming truly born again, you will have a new desire and hunger to follow after righteousness.No longer will you desire to follow after sin this time because you have the new nature of Christ in you that makes you hate the sin you once loved and love the righteousness you once hated.And if you are such a person who thirsts and desires righteousness, Jesus Christ said in **(Matthews 5:6)** that you are blessed indeed and you shall be filled with His righteousness.

15. Crucified Self.
Crucifying your sinful self will be one of the clear signs that will you if you become a genuine believer in the Lord Jesus Christ.

A person who has become a true Christian will crucify self and take up their cross daily to follow Christ even if it's inconvenient as true Christianity is all about self-denial and if you can't do that dear, you can't be a true follower of Christ.

No wonder the apostle Paul said in **(Galatians 2:20)** that He's crucified with Christ and not himself but Christ now lives in him and directs his life. This will be the case with you as well if you are a true Christian whose old sinful self has been Christ with Christ Jesus.

16. New Nature.
Last but not least having a new nature of Christ is among the most important signs of a true believer that a person will show if they experience genuine conversion.

This new nature of Christ Jesus will be as a result of the new birth one gets when they become genuinely born again after true repentance which leads to genuine salvation and eternal life.

It's this new nature Paul talks about in **(Colossians 3:10-20)** that will now enable you to live a holy life that's above sin. Without this new nature of Christ in you preset in all true believers, sin will be impossible for you to overcome.

Now we will consider these three influences which control the lives of unbelievers and still tempt believers.

1. Before Christ, believers followed the ways of this world.
When Paul says "world," he is not referring to the physical world but to the social value-system in the world, which is against God. The world is a system of thoughts and beliefs that contradict God and his Word. It is a system of groupthink, where everybody is expected to think the same. John Stott calls it "cultural bondage."It includes how people view success, beauty, family, riches, power, and life in general.

The world is trying to conform everybody into the same image and draw people away from following God. **(Romans 12:2)** says, "Do not conform any longer to the pattern of this world, but be transformed by the renewing of your mind. Then you will be able to test and approve what God's will is his good, pleasing and perfect will."

The world is trying to mold people into the same pattern. This shows up in many forms and ideologies. One of the major patterns in this world today is pluralism and relativism. It says, "You can believe anything you want to believe, and if it's good for you it's OK, as long as it doesn't hurt anybody else." The problem with this is that you lose absolutes. There is no real right or wrong except for believing in absolute truth. Sexual immorality is OK. Homosexuality is OK. Adultery is OK. Divorce is acceptable. But anything that claims to be absolute truth is wrong. In a society like this, Christianity becomes more and more marginalized and persecuted because it teaches "absolutes." One should not lie, steal, or cheat. Sexual immorality is wrong. Homosexuality is wrong. Christ is the only way to heaven. This claws at the world system and stirs it to anger because the world constantly aims to mold people, even believers, into its form.

However, those who have been truly saved, though still affected by the world, are not characterized by it. Again, Paul says, "you used to live [in disobedience] when you followed the ways of this world" **(Eph 2:2).** This means true believers no longer live according to the groupthink and cultural bondage of the world. They are different, and this will heap up persecution towards them. First **Peter 4:3-4** says,

For you have spent enough time in the past doing what pagans choose to do living in debauchery, lust, drunkenness, orgies, carousing and detestable idolatry. They think it strange that you do not plunge with them into the same flood of dissipation, and they heap abuse on you.

A true Christian will commonly find himself mocked, considered strange, or even persecuted. Others will say, "You don't want to get drunk on the weekend." "You don't have sex before marriage." "You won't help us cheat on this test." "You won't lie." "You don't curse." "What's wrong with you?" Believers will continually be considered strange because they no longer follow the ways of this world. In fact, John said this reality is a test of true salvation. , "Do not love the world or anything in the world. If anyone loves the world, the love of the Father is not in him." **(1John 2:15).**

When John says, "the love of the Father is not in him," he is saying this person is not saved. He does not love God. In fact, assurance of salvation is the very theme of the book **(cf. 1 John 5:13).**

Are you still following the ways of this world? Or has God changed you? Those who are born again no longer follow the ways of this world. As Paul says in **(Galatians 6:14),** "the world has been crucified to me, and I to the world."

2. Before Christ, believers followed the ways of the devil.
Not only did believers follow the way of the world before they knew Christ, but they also followed the ways of the devil. Paul said the Ephesians followed "the ruler of the kingdom of the air, the spirit who is now at work in those who are disobedient" **(Eph 2:2).** Now when

Paul talks about "the spirit who is now at work in those who are disobedient," he is not saying that every unbeliever is possessed. Scripture teaches that Satan is not omnipresent like God. He cannot be in more than one place at once. The way he works in unbelievers is by tempting them through the world system, demons, and the flesh to be disobedient to God.

Interpretation Question: What types of temptation does The devil use?

The devil Tempts People Through Lies.

In the first temptation, he lied to Eve, saying that if she ate of the tree she would be like God. He also implied that God lied to her and didn't want the best for her. This is true of Satan's work in the world system as well. It is a system built on lies. It says, "People must do this; they must do that; they must think this way; they must dress that way." It is a system based on the lies of the devil.

The devil Tempts People Through Fear.

Scripture says he is a roaring lion seeking whom he may devour **(1 Peter 5:8).** Lions roar to provoke fear in their prey. Satan tempts through fear, fear of the future, fear of the past, fear of what other people think. **Proverbs 29:25** says, "The fear of man is a snare." Through fear Satan handicaps people and keeps them from following God and doing his will.

The devil Tempts People Through The Love Of Money And Power.

When he tempted Jesus, he appeared to him and said, "If you bow down to me, I will give you all the kingdoms of this world" **(Matt 4:9).** This is exactly what the majority of the world is running after. They are seeking money and fame, and it keeps them away from following God, "For the love of money is a root of all kinds of evil. Some people, eager for money, have wandered from the faith and pierced themselves with many griefs."**(1 Timothy 6:10)**

Certainly, there are many other ways the enemy tempts people including "the lust of the flesh, the lust of the eyes, and the pride of life" **(1 John 2:16, KJV).**

Interpretation Question: What does Paul mean by the "ruler of the kingdom of the air"?

When Paul says this, he seems to be talking about something in the heavenly realms. Scripture teaches that Satan has innumerable demons following his bidding, and they have some type of rule in the heavenly realms. We get a clear picture of this in Daniel 10. Daniel, a Jewish administrator in Babylon, was fasting for three weeks, and during that time, he saw a vision of an angel. The angel told Daniel that he initially came to answer his prayer when he first prayed, but he was resisted by the Prince of Persia, referring to a demon ruling in that country (v. 13). The angel gave Daniel revelation, and then said he was leaving to fight with the Prince of Persia and that the Prince of Greece would come as well (v. 20).

Scripture teaches that Satan is the prince of this world **(John 12:31)** and the prince of demons **(Matt 9:34).** He works to control this world and the people in it, not only through the world system but through a hierarchy of demons.

Their place of rule is the heavenly realms the air.

Paul talks about this further in **(Ephesians 6:12)**when he says, "For our struggle is not against flesh and blood, but against the rulers, against the authorities, against the powers of this dark world and against the spiritual forces of evil in the heavenly realms."

Before Christ, we were not only following the world, but we were following the influence of the devil through his demons.

3. Before Christ, believers followed the lusts and desires of the flesh.
The final way believers were controlled and influenced to disobey God is through the flesh. When Paul said the flesh, he is not referring to the body. The body itself is neutral it can be used for good or bad. However, within our bodies, we have a "fallen nature" passed on from Adam. We have a nature full of lusts and desires for evil things. MacArthur says this about lusts and desires:

Epithumia (lusts) refers to strong inclinations and desires of every sort, not simply to sexual lust. Thelēma (desires) emphasizes strong willfullness, wanting and seeking something with great diligence. As with trespasses and sins, lusts and desires are not given to show their distinctiveness but their commonness. They are used synonymously to represent fallen man's complete orientation to his own selfish way.

We lust for sex outside of marriage, for wealth and power, for excessive food and sleep, etc. However, if we are now following Christ, we are no longer controlled by these desires because the power and control of the flesh was broken by Christ. **Romans 6:6-7** says, "For we know that our old self was crucified with him so that the body of sin might be done away with, that we should no longer be slaves to sin because anyone who has died has been freed from sin." These desires no longer control us, but they still tempt us and can become strongholds in our lives.

Application Question: How can a believer walk in daily victory over these forces?

Believers maintain this victory by battling. They battle to no longer be conformed to this world, but to be transformed by the renewing of their minds **(Romans 12:2).** They transform their minds by continually meditating on and practicing Scripture. They buffet their bodies and make them slaves through continual discipline **(1 Cor 9:27).** Paul says, "Discipline yourself unto godliness" **(1 Tim 4:7).** Through rigorous spiritual disciplines like meditating on Scripture, prayer, church fellowship, repentance and serving others, we control our flesh. Paul says, "Walk in the Spirit and you will not fulfill the lusts of the flesh" **(Gal 5:16).** Finally, we defeat the devil by relying on God's power. Nothing in our flesh will work. Paul tells these believers to be strong in the Lord and his mighty power to stand against the devil. They must put on the full armor of God—a daily righteous lifestyle to have victory **(Eph 6:10-18).**

The Five Evident Changes We Undergo As A True Believer

Change of Direction

When a person puts their faith in Jesus as a true believer, they have confessed their sin and decided in their mind to forsake their old way of life in the world and to follow Jesus into a brand new life.

Change of Focus

A true believer's life is no longer focused on pleasing or indulging themselves, but in pleasing God and obeying what Jesus says to do by His Spirit. Their relationship with God becomes the most important thing in their life.

Change of Purpose

A true believer wants to share their new found faith, to proclaim the gospel and share their personal testimony. A true believer wants to grow up in their faith from a spiritual infant to a mature and complete leader in the kingdom of God.

Change of Discipline

A true believer will study the bible to get to know God (his nature and character) and to understand God's plan and purpose for their life.

A true believer will spend time in prayer every day to lift up the needs of others who are important to them.

Change of Family

A true believer will want to participate in the local church, for worship, fellowship, service, spiritual growth and to evangelise other people. A true believer will use their spiritual gifts to serve and care for others in the body of Christ as their spiritual family.

Of course, all of these changes don't happen at once, but over time, these transformations will be apparent to everyone who knows them well.

Final Thoughts.

I hope that reading this chapter on the signs of true believer and hypocrisy will now help you understand what being a genuine believer in Christ is all about which isn't just about miracles.As we consider **(Ephesians 2:1-7),** we see characteristics of true believers. We see their past, their present, and their future, let's endeavour to learn from this

Chapter Three

Why Hypocrisy In The Church?

What is a Christian?

A Christian is someone who is undergoing a theological, moral, and social transformation a radical change in their thoughts, actions, and relationships. A Christian is someone who holds tight to the good news the truth that Jesus died in our place for our sins, a fact proven by His resurrection from the dead.

What Do We Mean By Christian Hypocrisy?

Often people outside Christianity see the faith not as good news but good deeds. By their definition, Christians are supposed to love people and feed people and help people not talk about sin and repentance and Jesus. I have found that often they say, "Christians are hypocrites because they're supposed to love everybody, and then they talk about sin. And that's not loving." But as a Christian, we answer, "That is loving." People point out my sin and help me get past it. I talk to them about their sin and assist them in finding forgiveness and freedom. That is how we love each other.

Bible scholar Larry Richards explains the concept of hypocrisy in the New Testament. He says:

"The Greek words hypokrinomai (appears once in the NT), hypokrisis (6 times in the NT), and hypokritēs (20 times in the NT) denote someone acting out the part of a character in a play. In Greek drama the actors held over their faces oversized masks painted to represent the character they were portraying. In life, the hypocrite is a person who masks his real self while he plays a part for his audience.

That background of the word "hypocrite" in Greek theatre makes for an amazingly concrete definition.

What Characterizes The Religious Hypocrite?

 In Matthew's Gospel (where 16 of the 27 occurrences of these Greek words occur) we note these things:

A hypocrite does not act spontaneously from the heart but with calculation, to impress observers **(Mt 6:1–3).**
A hypocrite thinks only of the external trappings of religion, ignoring the central, heart issues of love for God and others **(Mt 15:1–21).**
A hypocrite uses spiritual talk to hide base motives **(Mt 22:18–22).**
Jesus give us this warning that to the hypocrites of every age: "Woe to you" **(Mt 23:13, 15, 16, 23, 25, 27, 29)."**

For more insights study more on chapter two for the signs of an hypocrite.

Gospel from Ash Wednesday's Mass, Jesus gives an extended teaching on the problem of hypocrisy. You can read it here: Matthew 6 – On Hypocrisy. In the modern age we have tended to reduce the notion of hypocrisy to duplicity. The modern notion is that a hypocrite is someone who says one thing but does another, a person who is two-faced, who is inconsistent or phony. Jesus' teaching on Hypocrisy does not exclude this notion but is far richer.

The Biblical understanding enunciated by Jesus is rooted in the original meaning of the Greek word ὑποκριταί (hypokritai) which means "stage actors." At one level it is easy to see how this word has come to mean some one who is phony. For what they claim to be, they really are not, they are just acting a role. But when no one is looking (i.e. the audience is gone) they revert to their true self, which is some one quite different. But Jesus in his teaching here develops the understanding far more richly that shows how sad and poignant hypocrisy is, what its origin is and how it can be overcome.

Hypocrisy defined – In effect Jesus describes hypocrisy as the sad state of a person who reduces himself to being an actor on a stage, because he does not know God the Father. There are many people who live their life in a desperate search for human approval and applause. They discern their dignity and worth, not from God, (who is in effect a stranger to them), but from what other human beings think of them. They are willing to adapt themselves often in dramatic ways to win approval. They are willing to play many roles and wear many masks to give the audience what they want. They are like actors on a stage, who seek applause or perhaps laughter and approval. Notice the way Jesus describes the heart of hypocrisy:

Jesus said to his disciples: "Take care not to perform righteous deeds in order that people may see them;….The Lord goes on to say that they blow a trumpet so that others will see them giving alms, they pray ostentatiously so that others may see they are praying, and they alter their appearance so that others may see they are fasting.

The Heart Of Hypocrisy
Thus, the goal of such a person is to be seen. They are on stage and seek to ingratiate themselves to the audience and win applause. Hence they engage in some action "in order that people may see them." It is clear that this is

ultimately very sad. A lonely actor on a stage performing whatever role is required in order to win approval from the current audience. Their inner core or deepest self is repressed and replaced by the demands of others. This is the true heart of and description of hypocrisy.

Many take this desperate need for approval from others to very self destructive extremes. Many young people, due to peer pressure, will engage in dangerous and unhealthy practices to win approval. Some will drop out of school, join gangs and commit crimes. Others will drink heavily or use drugs. Still others will tattoo and pierce their bodies, engage in sexual activity before marriage, and do many risky things. The need for approval is often the deep drive that underlies this desperate behavior. But like actors on a stage seeking applause they rush to fill these rolls and wait for the applause and acceptance.

Adults too will often compromise core principles in order to fit in and be liked, gain promotions or earn access. Christians will hide their faith, playing the role of a secular modern in order to win approval. Some will act deceitfully to please a boss, others will gossip or engage in any number of sinful behaviors to ingratiate themselves to a group.

It is also clear that our modern notion of hypocrisy as duplicity, while incomplete, is not wrong either. Why does the hypocrite act inconsistently, often in a duplicitous manner? Because the audience changes, and he must change with it. So to one group he will say "yes" and to another group he will say "no." Since the goal of the hypocrite (actor) is to be seen and win approval, the answer must change if the group does. Hence he will morph, hide his true thoughts or outright lie to gain the approval. He no longer has a core, his identity is outside of himself in what ever the audience requires in order to grant him approval.

Why Then Are They Hypocrites In The Church?

Unfortunately, one obstacle to the acceptance of Christianity that is often raised is provided by Christians themselves. Phrased in many ways, the core of the objection is, "If Christianity is true, why are there hypocrites in the church?"

Like I've mentioned before, a hypocrite is someone who not only does not practice what one preaches, but a person who does the opposite of what one preaches. A parent holding a beer and smoking a cigarette who admonishes a child not to drink or smoke, for instance, may be viewed as being a hypocrite by the child.

Similarly, critics of Christianity who raise the hypocrisy objection usually point to some moral failure in the lives of Christians they know as examples of Christianity being false or at least highly suspect. "See!" they exclaim. "There goes another hypocrite in the church! How can I believe Christianity if the church is full of hypocrites?"

Before directly answering the question, we'll take a brief look at biblical examples of hypocrisy.

The Bible And Hypocrisy

"Hypocrisy" or variations of it appear 17 times in the NIV translation of the Bible. Often it is Christ calling people hypocrites (see, for instance, Matthew 6:2, 5, 16; 7:5; 15:7; 22:18; 23:13, 15; 23:23, 25, 27, 29; 24:51; Mark 7:6; Luke 6:42; 12:56; and 13:15). "You hypocrites!" in fact is a recurring phrase.

Some Of The Bible Verses As Related To Hypocrisy

(Matthew 7:1-5) is an important passage in regards to hypocrisy. Here Jesus tells those who would look for a speck in their brother's eye to consider the plank in their own. Judgmentalism typically accompanies hypocrisy. Often the sins we are most vocal about speaking against are the ones running wild within.

(Matthew 23:27-28) is part of Jesus' woes against the Pharisees. This entire section is a good place to look for visual pictures of hypocrisy as well as to consider how Jesus thinks about hypocrisy.

(Galatians 2:11-13) shows that even great Christian leaders like the apostle Peter can be given over to hypocrisy. Here he is rebuked by Paul for being a hypocrite. Peter believes the gospel, but his lifestyle doesn't match up to the implications of the gospel, and it is causing harm to others.

(1 Peter 2:1-3) tells us that hypocrisy is part the old man that needs to be cast aside. By craving the spiritual milk of the word, we will grow up into salvation and thereby be more consistent in our lifestyle.

Was Jesus guilty of pointing out the speck in someone else's eye when in fact he had a plank in his own? Not at all.

"Christianity does not stand or fall on the way Christians have acted throughout history or are acting today. Christianity stands or falls on the person of Jesus, and Jesus was not a hypocrite. He lived consistently with what He taught, and at the end of His life He challenged those who had lived with Him night and day, for over three years, to point out any hypocrisy in Him. His disciples were silent, because there was none.

Since Christianity depends on Jesus, it is incorrect to try to invalidate the Christian faith by pointing to horrible things done in the name of Christianity." Josh McDowell and Don Stewart, Answers to Tough Questions Skeptics Ask About the Christian Faith (Here's Life Publishers, 1980), 128.

McDowell and Stewart bring up three important points. First, whether or not Christianity is true does not depend on how its adherents behave. This, of course, does not excuse hypocrisy in the church, but neither does it mean that hypocrisy is sufficient reason to dismiss Christianity. Second, Christ was not a hypocrite in any sense of the word. Often even critics agree with this point, exalting the high moral standards of Christ without understanding His larger claims. Third, seemingly hypocritical behavior on a large scale, such as the Inquisition, does not invalidate Christianity, either. Again, this does not excuse hypocritical behavior, but separates it from the center of Christianity.

Are all Christians hypocrites? Not at all!

In fact, the history of the Christian church is filled with examples of selflessness, courage, moral action and reform and many other positive influences on the world. These are not the acts of hypocrites, but of sincere believers transformed by the resurrected Christ and moved by the Holy Spirit to "do to others what you would have them do to you" **(Matthew 7:12; Luke 6:31).**

The church is a work in progress (and so are its members). Like a cathedral that may take decades or centuries to complete, the process is long and arduous, but someday it will be complete and stand as a beautiful testimony to the power of Christ to transform lives for the better. Remember, too, that only some professing Christians act hypocritically. What about all those who do not? What about all those who consistently live out the love of Christ in the world?

Hypocrisy, Moral Standards, and Sin

Until the church and all followers of Christ are glorified, there will, unfortunately, be hypocrites in the church. What's important to remember, however, is that,
We must also remember that, biblically speaking, "all have sinned and fall short of the glory of God, and are justified freely by his grace through the redemption that came by Christ Jesus" **(Romans 3:23-24).** In other words, no one is perfect and all are dependent on Christ for redemption, salvation and growth in spiritual maturity. On the one hand, Christians should not act hypocritically, lest we provide critics with a flimsy reason to reject the gospel message. On the other hand, critics should know better than to attempt to throw out Christianity and all of Christ's claims on the basis of the hypocrisy objection.

Christian Hypocrisy, Jesus' Reaction

Combatting hypocrisy was a passion for Jesus. In fact, much of Matthew 23 is dedicated to this topic. Here are some excerpts:

"Then Jesus said to the crowds and to his disciples: 'The teachers of the law and the Pharisees sit in Moses' seat. So you must be careful to do everything they tell you. But do not do what they do, for they do not practice what they preach. They tie up heavy, cumbersome loads and put them on other people's shoulders, but they themselves are not willing to lift a finger to move them. Everything they do is done for people to see...

"'Woe to you, teachers of the law and Pharisees, you hypocrites! You clean the outside of the cup and dish, but inside they are full of greed and self-indulgence.

"'Woe to you, teachers of the law and Pharisees, you hypocrites! You are like whitewashed tombs, which look beautiful on the outside but on the inside are full of the bones of the dead and everything unclean. In the same way, on the outside you appear to people as righteous but on the inside you are full of hypocrisy and wickedness.'"

Jesus took hypocrisy very seriously. Mark Mittleberg says, "Our friends naturally see Christians' hypocritical behavior as being unacceptable. But they need help to see that Christ feels the same way."2 They need to see that they agree with Jesus on this one!

Christian Hypocrisy – Some Pointers

When discussing Christian hypocrisy with an unbeliever, here are some pointers to consider:

Many people who claim to be Christians don't have a personal relationship with Jesus Christ. Perhaps they are Christian in name only.

A Christian is called to grow in faith and progress to being more like Christ. This doesn't always happen instantly. Many Christians continue to struggle with temptation to sin. We are called to put on a new nature and allow the Holy Spirit to transform our lives **(Ephesians 4:23-24).** It is not hypocritical to fall. It is hypocritical to deny that you fell and pretend that you were successful.

A Christian is called to live a life of compassion, kindness, humility, gentleness, and patience **(Colossians 3:12).** Be intentional about letting God change your heart. Christians should admit hypocrisy. All of us are hypocrites in some area. Be vulnerable, honest, and authentic with unbelievers. Acknowledge your sin and share how freeing God's forgiveness is.

Why does this happen to a person?

Here too Jesus is rather clear. This happens to a person who does not know God the Father. The great tragedy of many lives is that they do not know the Father. They may know about God, but they do not personally know God or his love for them. God is at best a benevolent stranger who runs the universe but he is in some remote heaven and the interaction that many have with him is vague and abstract. God exists but he is on the periphery of life. In effect he is a stranger.

Notice the remedy that Jesus assigns for each example of hypocrisy he cites:

Your heavenly Father, who sees in secret will repay you for giving alms….Your heavenly Father who sees in secret will repay you for praying…..Your heavenly Father who sees what is hidden will repay you for your fasting.

In other words the goal in life and the remedy for hypocrisy is that it is enough that Your heavenly Father sees what you do. Now of course, as long as God the Father remains a distant and aloof figure what he sees never will be enough for us. But to the degree that we begin to experience God the Father's love for us, his providence and his good will toward us, then we become less concerned with what others think. We begin to come down off the stage and be less concerned for the approval of men and more focused on and then satisfied with the approval of God.

Notice too the intimacy that Jesus sets forth. He says of God, He is "Your heavenly Father." He is not merely the "Deity." He is not merely God in heaven. He is not even merely the Father. He is "YOUR heavenly Father." He is the one who created you, sustains you, provides for and loves you.

To conclude, we can learn a lot from this statement from Mark Mittleberg: "The primary issue regarding the validity of Christianity is not Jesus' followers but Jesus himself and what he offers to those who follow him. Ultimately we need to encourage our friends to put their faith not in Christianity and certainly not in the flawed efforts of frail Christians but in the powerful and proven person of Jesus Christ himself."

Chapter Four

The Hypocrisy of Self-Righteousness – John 8:1-11

Even in ancient Rome the hypocrite was despised. Cicero wrote, "Of all villainy, there is none more base than that of the hypocrite, who, at the moment he is false, takes care to appear most virtuous." Hypocrisy comes in many varieties, but the worst kind is self-righteous hypocrisy. What is even more tragic about this kind of hypocrisy is that the practitioner is often not even aware of it.

Self-righteousness is the worst disease to ever afflict the human race. Self-righteousness will keep you from grace and lock you out of the kingdom.
For this reason, great preachers like "Martin Luther and Charles Spurgeon" made a habit of preaching against self-righteousness.

But do you know what self-righteousness is?

Do you recognize its symptoms?

What Is Self-Righteousness?

Self-righteousness is trusting in your own righteousness **(Luke 18:9).** It is believing there are things you can do to make yourself right with God.

Self-righteousness is sometimes manifested in feelings of superiority towards others. "I am right, you are wrong. My way is better than your way."

But self-righteousness can also be reflected in a low sense of self-worth ("God can't possibly love me"), an inflated sense of self-importance ("I need to do more for God"), and outright unbelief ("I am beyond the reach of his grace").

That **"holier-than-thou"** attitude some people exhibit can get pretty annoying. But self-righteousness goes even deeper than that when you consider it from the theological point of view. In a sense, there isn't a righteous person on the planet right now, and if you believe in God, only He can have that attribute.

Here are some crucial facts that should help you understand whether you're on a good path or perhaps have a superiority complex you need to deal with.

What Does It Mean to Be Self-Righteous?

Fortunately, there are many dictionaries online that could give you an idea of what self-righteousness is.

Collins dictionary points out that self-righteous people are convinced they are right when it comes to their behavior, beliefs, and attitudes. Oxford takes it to the next level with its definition, saying that self-righteous people always believe they are morally right and everyone else is, of course, wrong.

Cambridge dictionary says something similar again. Self-righteous people are, according to Cambridge, those who believe they are morally better than others. Meanwhile, Merriam-Webster goes a bit further, adding that self-righteous people are narrow-mindedly moralistic.

Overall, it all boils down to a simple notion: self-righteousness is a trait of people who believe they are morally or otherwise above others. It is, above all, a holier-than-thou attitude that makes someone intolerant of others' opinions, beliefs, and behaviors.

Examples Of People In The Bible Who Displayed Self Righteousness

- The first example is King Solomon. Although the Wisdom of Solomon was world-renowned, Solomon had one downfall. He had too many wives, many who were from other countries and therefore had their own gods and demanded proper worship from Solomon. This ultimately went against God's commands. In **(1 Kings 11),** we see this to its full extent:

The Lord did not want the Israelites to worship foreign gods, so he had warned them not to marry anyone who was not from Israel… As Solomon got older, some of his wives led him to worship their gods. He wasn't like his father David, who had worshiped only the Lord God. Solomon also worshiped Astarte the goddess of Sidon, and Milcom the disgusting god of Ammon. Solomon's father had obeyed the Lord with all his heart, but Solomon disobeyed and did what the Lord hated. Solomon built shrines on a hill east of Jerusalem to worship Chemosh the disgusting god of Moab, and Molech the disgusting god of Ammon. In fact, he built a shrine for each of his foreign wives, so all of them could burn incense and offer sacrifices to their own gods.

- The second example is the Prophet Jonah. Jonah was at the top of his game as Israel's prophet. But when God called him to the unthinkable, Jonah thought he could run and hide from the Creator of the Universe.

Even after everything he went through (remember the fish), he was surprised that the Ninevites repented and turned to the Lord. He was so upset that God did not spite such wicked people, that God showed them mercy and grace. This can be seen in **(Jonah 1:1-3),**

One day the Lord spoke to Jonah son of Amittai. He said, "Go to Nineveh, that great city, and speak out against it; I am aware of how wicked its people are." Jonah, however, set out in the opposite direction in order to get away from the Lord. He went to Joppa, where he found a ship about to go to Spain. He paid his fare and went aboard with the crew to sail to Spain, where he would be away from the Lord.

- The third example is the Sanhedrin. These were the people who gave false evidence against Jesus because they were too proud to accept that they had faults and were not representing the Lord their God as they were called, as stated in **(Matthew 26:57-67),**

"Those who had arrested Jesus took him to Caiaphas the high priest, where the teachers of the law and the elders had assembled. But Peter followed him at a distance, right up to the courtyard of the high priest. He entered and sat down with the guards to see the outcome. The chief priests and the whole Sanhedrin were looking for false evidence against Jesus so that they could put him to death."

- The fifth example is the Pharisees, one of the most famous examples of self-righteous people. Jesus always made an example of self-righteousness, and one of the most renowned parables He told was about the Pharisees, as stated in **(Luke 18:10-14),**

"Two men went up to the temple to pray, one a Pharisee and the other a tax collector. The Pharisee stood by himself and prayed: 'God, I thank you that I am not like other people robbers, evildoers, adulterers or even like this tax collector.

I fast twice a week and give a tenth of all I get.' But the tax collector stood at a distance. He would not even look up to heaven but beat his breast and said, 'God, have mercy on me, a sinner.' I tell you that this man, rather than the other, went home justified before God. For all those who exalt themselves will be humbled, and those who humble themselves will be exalted."

- And the last and one of the best examples of relying on self-righteousness is the Apostle Peter. Who could forget Peter's assurance to Jesus that He would never betray Him only to betray Him three times in a row, as stated in **(Luke 22:58-62),**

But Peter said, "Man, I am not." And after an interval of about an hour still another insisted, saying, "Certainly this man also was with him, for he too is a Galilean." But Peter said, "Man, I do not know what you are talking about." And immediately, while he was still speaking,

the rooster crowed. And the Lord turned
and looked at Peter. And Peter
remembered the saying of the Lord, how
he had said to him, "Before the rooster
crows today, you will deny me three
times." And he went out and wept
bitterly."

What Causes Self-Righteousness?

It is easy to see how your focus on yourself can
be the primary cause of self-righteousness.
Inside your mind, you are the main character.
Everything else around you almost seems like a
sitcom episode if you're lucky or a thriller in
some cases.

But the reasons for someone becoming self-
righteous are mostly tied to irrational thoughts.
One of them is the black-or-white perception
something is either this or that, and there's
nothing else in between. This causes you to
never broaden your mind (something self-
righteous people are notorious for). Instead, you
restrict yourself to believing that the opposite of
perfect (the maximum) is an utter failure (the
minimum).

Self-righteous people also dabble in overgeneralizations a lot, especially when it comes to negative experiences. They use radical words like always and never that are extremely limiting. There isn't anything above always or below never, so these are, once again, two extremes self-righteousness thrives on.

Fear, Insecurity, And The Anxiety They Produce

Another reason you may become self-righteous is insecurity that stems from fear and anxiety. Self-righteous people often feel as if they are under attack. If you don't agree with them, you are definitely against them.

A person that can rationally think things through and come to a conclusion based on facts, logic, and consideration doesn't have anything to be self-righteous about. They understand the topic at hand thoroughly, so they can be confident not so much about them being right but about their capacity of thinking.

They may not have followed the easiest road to a conclusion, and they may have made mistakes

along the way. However, they self-corrected
until they got a firm grasp on a certain notion.

Self-righteous people don't do that because they
aren't sure of their logic and way of thinking.
Unfortunately, that causes a lack of inner peace
that makes them turn to persuasion and even
intimidation to prove they are, in fact, right
about things.If others come to the side, they will
get evidence their behavior, thoughts, and
beliefs are superior to others. There's no need to
prove them through rational thought, as they
win by numbers in that case (no matter how
hollow the victory is).

Self-righteousness can sometimes display itself
in almost humorous ways such as in the
following story. A pastor and his assistant were
practicing for a service. In order to make his
point dramatic, the preacher fell to his knees,
beat his breast and said, "I am nothing. I am
nothing!" The associate was so moved by this
that he too fell to his knees and cried, "I am
nothing. I am nothing!" The janitor heard and
saw this and was so moved by it that he too fell
to his knees and cried, "I am nothing. I am
nothing!" When the minister heard the janitor,

he turned to his associate and said, "So look who has the gall to think he is nothing."

The obviousness of this makes it humorous, but the reality is that such hypocrisy is, as John R. W. Stott described it (Sermon on the Mount), a cancerous killing agent. He went on to say, "Unfortunately, hypocrisy is also addictive. And even though Jesus reserved His most severe words of condemnation for the hypocrite, we still seem to prefer that lifestyle to truth and authenticity."

This text gives a clear example of the self-righteous hypocrisy of the Jewish religious leaders as they try to entrap Jesus. He not only avoids their trap, but He also exposes their hypocrisy, though in a relatively gentle manner. Turn to **(John 8:1-11).** Let us take warning from this passage the danger of falling into the hypocrisy of self-righteousness and also learn how to be gracious in dealing with both hypocrites and those entrapped in sin.

Papias, a disciple of John, makes reference to a story of a woman accused of many sins before the Lord which may explain its addition into later copies of John's gospel account.

I am going to treat the passage as belonging here because I would rather error on the side of including it than excluding it and even more so since the evidence backs it up as a genuine incident in the life of Christ. The passage fits in with the flow of John's presentation here and it teaches a valuable lesson on how to deal with people.

The Context – **John 7 & 8:1-2**

This incidence appears to have taken place at the conclusion of the Feast of Booths. Recall from our previous studies that Jesus had come down from Galilee to Jerusalem sometime during the middle of the feast. He came without drawing attention to Himself, but after He arrived He continued His normal practice of teaching the people. While He was teaching, some of the Jews that are hostile to Him made disparaging remarks which in turn led to Jesus challenging them about their plot to kill Him. (See: Judging with Righteous Judgment) By the time the debate is over, there is a mixture of beliefs about Jesus among the people. Some think He is the promised prophet of Deuteronomy 18 who would be like Moses. Some think He is the promised Messiah. Others claim Jesus cannot be the Messiah and is a deceiver of some kind, and most of the religious leaders have rejected Jesus and have joined in plotting to kill Him.

The end of John 7 records that the Pharisees were so upset that they were belittling everyone that disagreed with them and making false outrageous claims. They who claimed to be the keepers of the Mosaic Law and teacher of God's word were breaking it and continued to do so even when Nicodemus, who was a Pharisee, specifically pointed out their infraction.

(John 7:53) concludes with everyone returning to their own homes. **John 8:1** states that "Jesus went to the Mount of Olives." This is a favorite place for Jesus to go and it is also a logical place for pilgrims to be stay. The restrictions placed on travel during a Sabbath made the Mount of Olives, which was just opposite the

Kidron Valley from the temple, a good place to camp.

Verse 2 begins, "Early in the morning He came again into the Temple." The word here (o[rqroV / orthros) actually indicates the dawning or "daybreak." If the previous day, which was the "great day of the feast" (7:37), was the seventh day of the feast, this would be the eighth day which was a prescribed Sabbath day that followed the Feast of Booths **(Numbers 29:35).** There are a large number of pilgrims still in Jerusalem as well as the native inhabitants. Verse 2 continues, "and all the people were coming to Him; and He sat down and began to teach them."

Jesus continued His ministry of teaching people about God and the Scriptures. This was the ministry He began several years earlier and had continued ever since **(Matthew 4:23).** As the morning progresses more and more people are coming to the temple and are joining in the crowd listening to Jesus teach.Just as on previous occasions, the religious leaders are not happy when someone else is getting the attention they want. They are a jealous lot and they do not like Jesus. However, they have rapidly developing problem. As Jesus gains respect and popularity by His teaching, they will have a harder time arresting Him without arousing the anger of the people. They have to find a way to discredit Him. They have already tried the direct approach by disparaging Jesus and mocking Him for not having the right credentials to teach (7:15). They had tried arresting Jesus the day before (7:32), but that did not work either for the officers refused to do so for they were so impressed by Jesus' teaching, commenting, "Never has a man spoken the way this man speaks" (7:46). They will now attempt to discredit Jesus through a test case designed to trap him so that they could accuse Him.

The Test – **John 8:3-6**

John 8:3, And the scribes and the Pharisees ^brought a woman caught in adultery, and having set her in the midst, 4 they ^said to Him, "Teacher, this woman has been caught in adultery, in the very act. 5 "Now in the Law Moses commanded us to stone such women; what then do You say?" 6 And they were saying this, testing Him, in order that they might have grounds for accusing Him

It is interesting to note here that the scribes have joined in with the Pharisees in this plot. The scribes were the religious lawyers, and since Judea was a religious society, they were very powerful. Theologically, the scribes tended to be Sadducees. The Sadducees were the liberals of the day who denied the miraculous along with Angels and Demons. They approached life from a rationalistic perspective. Usually the scribes and Pharisees were in opposition to one another, but here they join forces because Jesus has become a common enemy to both.

Judea was under Roman rule with Roman law as the final authority in the nation with a Roman governor (or procurator) present to enforce it. Yet, the Roman government gave the nations and local governments under them quite a bit of control over the daily affairs of society. The Sanhedrin was the ruling council of the nation. It was made up of seventy elders, and most of them were either scribes or Pharisees. This test case needed the cooperation of both because it was a case that should have been brought to the

Sanhedrin. They had counseled together to set the case before Jesus first as a means to entrap Him.

The scribes and Pharisees bring a woman before Jesus and then take on the role of prosecutors. Their design is to discredit Jesus in front of the people, but there is the risk of it backfiring for it places Jesus in the role of judge, an acknowledgment of Jesus' importance as a teacher. The fact that they are risking this shows how self-confident they were that they could find a ground of accusation against Jesus that would severely damage His reputation and enable them to persecute Him and perhaps even bring Him to trial.

The case appeared to be straight forward. They publically accuse the woman of adultery claiming to have caught her in the very act. They then cite the relevant part of the Mosaic law. Leviticus 20:10 states, "If there is a man who commits adultery with another man's wife, one who commits adultery with his friend's wife, the adulterer and the adulteress shall surely be put to death." It does not matter whether this woman was married or not, though the specific accusation indicates she was married, for the sin and penalty were the same. The usual method of execution for adultery was stoning which was also the prescribed method for fornication **(Deuteronomy 22:21).**

Their purpose in bringing this matter before Jesus is clearly stated in verse 6. They were testing Jesus so that they might have grounds for accusing Him. They were looking for a way to bring an official charge against Jesus so that He could be condemned by the Sanhedrin. They were familiar enough with Jesus' teaching to know both His compassion and how He would forgive people their sins **(Luke 5:20; 7:48).** They expected that Jesus would end up being in opposition to the very clear and direct command of Moses. This would be their charge against Him. It has been pointed out by some that the common people were not very favorable to stoning for adultery, but what sinner is in favor of a punishment they may suffer? Perhaps that thought was in the back of their minds as sort of a "win – win" situation. If Jesus advised she not be stoned they would charge Him with opposing the law of Moses, and if He advised stoning her, then Jesus would lose some popularity with the crowds. However, the text is clear that their effort was to find grounds for accusing Him.

This may be the reason they did not bring the man with them. Note again in verse 4 that the woman was caught in the very act of adultery. That means the man was also present. Some have suggested that he ran away and they were only able to catch the woman. I find that idea to be a bit of a stretch since there is an emphasis that they were caught in the very act of adultery. The hypocrisy of these Scribes and Pharisees is demonstrated in the fact that the man is not present, yet they are prosecuting the woman. Even if the man had run away, what was to prevent them from finding him and then charging him too? But this is in keeping with their hypocritical character. They are not interested in carrying out the Mosaic Law themselves. Their interest is only in trying to entrap Jesus and they do not need the man to do that. In addition, perhaps they thought that Jesus would have more compassion on a woman than a man and thus more likely to end up opposing the Mosaic law. Simon the Pharisee was present when Jesus had on a former occasion forgiven a prostitute **(Luke 7:39-50).**

The Solution – **(John 8:6-11)**

Jesus' response is not one they could have anticipated. The end of verse 6 states, "But Jesus stooped down, and with His finger wrote on the ground." There is no indication as to what Jesus was writing, who He was writing to or why He was writing. Basically, Jesus ignores them and their demand for a judgment. His silence toward them was probably deafening. Imagine being in a court room after the case is presented and the judge suddenly becomes silent and seems preoccupied in writing something. It is possible, if not probable, that Jesus was writing something directed to them, but verse 7 indicates that they were not paying attention to it if He was. They wanted an answer to their question.

7 But when they persisted in asking Him, He straightened up, and said to them, "He who is without sin among you, let him [be the] first to throw a stone at her." 8 And again He stooped down, and wrote on the ground."

Jesus is busy writing something on the ground with His finger and you can almost hear the desperation rising in their voices as they persist in asking what should be done to the woman. It would have been a demand for attention from someone who was seemingly ignoring them. Keep in mind that it is the superior that can ignore the inferior and not the other way around. Jesus will answer in His own timing and not theirs.

When Jesus does answer, it is in a way that again demonstrates His superiority to them. In courtesy and majesty He stands up from being stooped over and writing on the ground and addresses them, and then He goes back to writing on the ground. He gives His decision and then returns to what He had been doing before. Jesus' charge to them was shocking. "He who is without sin among you, let him [be the] first to throw a stone at her."

They never expected such an answer from Jesus. It gave them nothing with which to accuse Jesus as being against the Mosaic Law and it put the responsibility right back on their shoulders with a condition that none of them could meet. That Jesus told them to carry out the requirement of the law should not have been surprising. **(Deuteronomy 17:6-7)** clearly states how capital punishment was to be carried out. "On the evidence of two witnesses or three witnesses, he who is to die shall be put to death; he shall not be put to death on the evidence of one witness. 7 "The hand of the witnesses shall be first against him to put him to death, and afterward the hand of all the people. So you shall purge the evil from your midst."

Executions under the Mosaic Law were not affairs removed from the public to some hidden place and carried out by a government official using some quick means of death. Executions were carried out in public by the public starting with those who witnessed the crime, and stoning was a dreadful way to die. Since these scribes and Pharisees were accusing the woman and claimed to have caught her in the act. They were both the prosecutors and witnesses, so it was their responsibility to start the execution process. Her blood would be on their hands. I don't know if that in itself would have bothered them so much. They certainly had the blood of many others on their hands and the were trying to find a way to kill Jesus. What bothered them was the condition Jesus placed on them. The execution was to begin by whoever was without sin among the accusers casting the first stone. They could not meet that condition and they knew it.

Jesus returned to writing in the dirt with His finger. Again, there is no indication what He was writing. Perhaps it was a list of various sins they had done. Perhaps it was aspects of the Mosaic Law they had broken. Perhaps it was doodling or figures of some sort. We do not know what Jesus wrote, but we do know the immediate effect of what Jesus said and was doing had on the scribes and Pharisees.

(John 8:9), "And when they heard it, they [began] to go out one by one, beginning with the older ones, and He was left alone, and the woman, where she was, in the midst."

Some have suggested that the reason that they left one by one starting with the oldest was that the oldest was the most aware of their own sins. Perhaps that is possible, but I don't think that is what is happening because I have found that older people who continue in sin become more hardened in it. These men demonstrated both before and after this event that they were very hardened in their own sin. I am not even sure that these men are leaving because they are convicted of their own sin, but more that they realize that Jesus has escaped their trap and that if they push any farther on this it is going to go from bad to worse for them. Jesus had already publically accused them of plotting to kill Him and many of the Jerusalemites were aware of this plot (7:19, 25). They did not personally meet the criteria and if they stayed around any longer they risked this accusation being brought up again by a man to whom they had just given tacit approval as someone whose judgment was worth seeking. The charge of adultery is serious, but not nearly so as a charge of plotting a murder.

I think their manner of departure has more to do with the older ones recognizing the defeat first and the decorum of the younger showing respect for those who are older. In fact, the term "older" here is "elder" and could even refer to those who were part of the Sanhedrin. The younger let their superiors leave first as a sign of respect.

The Application –**(John 8:10-11)**

A point generally overlooked in this is Jesus' manner of dealing with these opponents in a gracious manner. While Jesus does not give any deference to the scribes and Pharisees, He is still generally courteous to them. Jesus quickly took the superior position in this incident, yet He did not use it to strike out against His opponents. Jesus' statement is confrontational, but He could have been very direct in exposing their hypocrisy by bringing specific charges against them for the various aspects of the Mosaic law they were breaking, chief among them the plot to kill Him. Yet, Jesus is gracious and gives them room to retreat.

Our human desire for vengeance would have driven most of us to take advantage of the situation to humiliate our opponents. Jesus gives grace. Be honest, if it had been you, would you have enjoyed the opportunity of damaging your adversary? Jesus gave grace. It is a point for each of us to consider and follow Jesus' example.

(Psalm 145:8) declares, "The Lord is gracious and merciful; Slow to anger and great in lovingkindness." This is the character of Jesus. It is also to be a character each of us is called to emulate. Consider the following Scriptures: **(Proverbs 16:32),** "He who is slow to anger is better than the mighty, And he who rules his spirit, than he who captures a city." **(Proverbs 14:29),** "He who is slow to anger has great understanding, But he who is quick-tempered exalts folly." Proverbs 15:1, "A gentle answer turns away wrath, But a harsh word stirs up anger." **(2 Timothy 2:24-26),** "24 And the Lord's bond-servant must not be quarrelsome, but be kind to all, able to teach, patient when wronged, 25 with gentleness correcting those who are in opposition, if perhaps God may grant them repentance leading to the knowledge of the truth, 26 and they may come to their senses [and escape] from the snare of the devil, having been held captive by him to do his will."

We do not win people to the Lord by debate and backing our opponents into a corner. We win them through being examples of Jesus Christ. If you are having a discussion with someone, do not back away from the truth for Jesus did not, yet do not to seek to destroy your opponent either, for that is also Jesus' example. Give them some room to retreat with some dignity. They may not take it, as we will see in future studies in John's gospel, but you can at least make an escape route available if they will take it. This works with your children too. Certainly you are to be clear and direct in teaching them right from wrong, but when they have done something wrong there is no benefit in berating them. Give them some room to retreat with some dignity still left. If Jesus could do that with these hypocritical Scribes and Pharisees, then we can do it with our children and also our opponents.

The scribes and Pharisees retreated leaving Jesus alone with the woman in the midst. The indication here is that these religious rulers had left, but the crowd Jesus had been teaching remained. The woman is in the midst of this crowd, but alone with Jesus in the sense that Jesus is left alone to deal with her. Again we find Him to be most merciful and gracious.

(John 8:10-11), "And straightening up, Jesus said to her, "Woman, where are they? Did no one condemn you?" 11 And she said, "No one, Lord." And Jesus said, "Neither do I condemn you; go your way. From now on sin no more."

After the Scribes and Pharisees left, Jesus stood up again and addressed the woman directly. Jesus' question to her was not whether anyone had accused her, but whether anyone had condemned her. Jesus had heard the accusation, but none of those who accused were willing to condemn with the conditions Jesus had placed on them. As I pointed out earlier from **(Deuteronomy 17:6),** condemnation required two or three witnesses. One witness was insufficient. And in this case, there were no witnesses left.

What an example of grace given to a sinner. All who would doubt that God could forgive them can have those doubts removed here. God is gracious to the humble. It really does not matter what sins you have committed, forgiveness can be found in Jesus Christ. Adultery, fornication, lying, coveting, stealing, envy, hatred, murder, idolatry, blasphemy whatever you have done or failed to do. Jesus Christ can forgive you leaving none left to condemn you. What a beautiful truth this is as expressed by the Apostle Paul in **(Romans 8:1)** which wonderfully proclaims, "There is therefore now no condemnation for those who are in Christ Jesus."

Salvation from sin is a gift of God's grace through faith in Jesus Christ. **(Ephesians 2:8-9)** states it this way, "For by grace you have been saved through faith; and that not of yourselves, [it is] the gift of God; 9 not as a result of works, that no one should boast." You don't deserve it and you cannot earn it. It comes simply by placing your faith in Jesus Christ which we have pointed out before means to believe Jesus' claims about Himself and what He has done. He is the eternal creator God in human flesh who lived a sinless life and then died a sin sacrifice as your substitute and then rose from the dead the third day. He ascended to heaven and is preparing a place for His followers, and He will return to receive us to Himself.

But I must point out lest there be any misunderstanding of what such a belief requires. It means a sinner is forgiven. It comes while you are still a sinner. You cannot clean up your life enough to be worthy of it. But it will change the way you live from that point on.

Notice in verse 11 that while Jesus does not condemn the woman, neither does He ignore her sin. His charge to her, "from now on sin no more," is a very direct recognition that she has sinned and that she needs to stop. But that is what salvation is about. It is not fire insurance, though escaping hell is a wonderful benefit. Salvation is from sin. It is about a change of masters from sin, self and Satan to the Lord Jesus Christ (see Romans 6).

Do not trample on the precious blood of Jesus which was shed for you by thinking that you can merrily continue in your sin after salvation. Yes, you will struggle against sin after salvation, but it is no longer master. If your life has not changed and you are not fighting against sin, then there is good reason to question what you really believe. Examine yourself to see if you are in the faith, that Jesus Christ is in you unless you fail the test **(2 Corinthians 13:5).** If you have doubts, a purpose of the church is to help you walk with Christ. Talk to one of the leaders or someone you know and let us help.

There is no condemnation to those who are in Christ Jesus. Are you in Him? 1 **(John 5:12)** declares, "He who has the Son has the life, he who does not have the Son does not have the life." Do you have the Son? Those who have the Son have changed masters **(Romans 6:22).** What master does your life indicate you are serving**. (Romans 6:16).**

An author wrote the following thought provoking poem describing self-righteous hypocrisy.
You call Me Master and obey Me not,
You call Me Light and see Me not,
You call Me Way and follow Me not,
You call Me Life and desire me not,
You call Me wise and acknowledge Me not,
You call Me fair and love Me not,
You call Me rich and ask Me not,
You call Me eternal and seek Me not,
You call Me gracious and trust me not,
You call Me noble and serve Me not,

You call Me mighty and honor Me not,
You call Me just and fear Me not,
If I condemn you, blame Me not

If you believe the truth about Jesus, then your life will change to conform to those beliefs. Don't not be a hypocrite like the scribes and Pharisees described in our text today. God resists the proud, but He gives grace to the humble **(James 4:6).**

Signs Of Self-Righteousness

Do you know that you can be self-righteous without even knowing it?

"Christians Are Called To Live A Righteous Life". However, there is one particular type of "righteousness" that can easily prevent us from entering the Kingdom of God. In fact, this kind of righteousness had been heavily condemned by our Lord and Savior, Jesus Christ. It is also the reason that Job was punished by God. This deceptive type of righteousness is so potent that it can easily spiritually blind a person and not even know that they have it.

It's Self-Righteousness. This problem has been a common sin throughout the history of the Church. After all, it is so easy to be self-righteous. It is a human and natural inclination that we all need to overcome.

Do you suppose this, O man, when you pass judgment on those who practice such things and do the same yourself, that you will escape the judgment of God? –**(Romans 2:3)**

In Romans 2, Paul explored this question: why is the self-righteous person guilty before God? First, Paul said, he is guilty because of his condemnation of others. Second, Paul said, he is guilty because of his hypocritical conduct. "Therefore you have no excuse, everyone of you who passes judgment, for in that which you judge another, you condemn yourself; for you who judge practice the same things. And we know that the judgment of God rightly falls upon those who practice such things. But do you suppose this, O man, when you pass judgment on those who practice such things and do the same yourself, that you will escape the judgment of God?" (2:1-3). The self-righteous person is guilty because he condemns activity in others that he condones in himself. Such a person will not escape God's judgment.

Paul was not saying you can never speak out against any sin that you have committed yourself. Look at Paul's own example. Paul was a blasphemer, a persecutor, and a murderer of Christians; he called himself in **(1 Timothy 1:15)** the chief of all sinners. Yet Paul spoke out against sin. Here is the difference: Paul confessed his sin, and he found the forgiveness of Jesus Christ. He repented; he turned away from his sin. He did not condemn sin in others that he condoned in his own life, and the same is true for you and me. Sometimes those who have committed a sin are in the best position to speak out against that sin once they have repented. Paul was saying, "Do not have two standards–one by which you judge others, and one by which you judge yourself. You will not escape the judgment of God."

The self-righteous person engages in selective obedience. He thinks, "As long as I am not guilty of this, then I am okay with God." The problem is, God does not grade on a curve. God demands 100% compliance with His law. In **(Galatians 3:10),** Paul said, "For as many as are of the works of the Law are under a curse; for it is written, 'Cursed is everyone who does not abide by all things written in the book of the law, to perform them.'" James said the same thing: "For whoever keeps the whole law and yet stumbles in one point, he has become guilty of all. For He who said, 'Do not commit adultery,' also said, 'Do not commit murder.' Now if you do not commit adultery, but do commit murder, you have become a transgressor of the law" (2:10-11).

Think of God's law as one of those huge chains that are used to keep an ocean liner in dock. Imagine one of those chains has 660 links in it, the number of God's laws. What happens if just one of those links in the chain is broken? It sets the entire ship adrift. That is what James was saying. If you keep 659 of God's laws, but break one of them, you are guilty of breaking all of God's law. You say, "That is impossible! Who can keep all of God's law?" Exactly. We all stand in need of the grace of God, but the self-righteous person does not understand that.

What Then Are The Signs Of A Self Righteous Person?

Sign 1;

Self-righteous people repel others.
Have you ever been around a person who made you feel uncomfortable, unrighteous, and guilty because you can see how he obviously show his righteousness? This person constantly rubs on your face his righteous acts and in the process, unconsciously "put people down". As a result, you don't like to make friends with this person because he has this aura of making you feel spiritually inferior.

That's exactly what self-righteousness does. It repels people. On the other hand, genuine righteousness draws people toward you. Jesus Christ is the perfect example of a righteous Being. He draws people toward Him and not fend them off.

Sign 2;

Self-Righteous People Parade Their Good Works.

The Pharisees and scribes are the perfect epitomia of self-righteousness. For that reason, Christ ardently reprimanded them. Read Matthew 23, and you will see how many times Christ said, "Woe to you, Scribes and Pharisees." Christ stated that we must exceed the righteousness of these people if ever we want to enter the Kingdom of God **(Matthew 5:20).**

Self-righteousness is more of the outward manifestation rather than an inward conversion of the person.

So what's wrong with the Pharisees and Scribes? They love to publicly display their righteousness to people. They were "wearing their righteousness outwardly." When they fast, they want to appear to people fasting **(Matthew 6:16).** When they repent, they don't produce the fruit of repentance **(Matthew 3:8).** When they give alms, they sound a trumpet **(Matthew 6:2).** And the list just goes on and on.

You get the point. Self-righteousness is more of the outward manifestation rather than an inward conversion of the person.

Sign 3;
Self-Righteous People Are Uncompassionate

Being self-righteous makes you a person without much compassion. Why? Because you see other people full of sins and faults and you don't understand why they are that way. You have a hard time looking into yourself and realizing that you also have a lot of unchecked problems Instead of being compassionate, self-righteous people are very critical of others.

Sign 4;
Self-Righteous People Hate And Condemn Sinners

Whenever you are in the presence of a thief, adulterer, extortionist, or somebody who have committed a horrible sin, does it make you feel uncomfortable? A self-righteous person hates sinners instead of just hating their sins.

Jesus Chris ate with tax collectors and talked to them. He spent more time with the perceived sinful people in His day than the Pharisees who are thought to be "righteous."

The danger with self-righteousness is it makes you believe that you are in the position of God. You condemn people and pass permanent judgment. You determine who will be part of God's kingdom and who will not.

True righteousness loves the sinner but hates the sin.

Sign 5;
Self-Righteous People Love The Approval And Praises Of Men

Among the motivations of a self-righteous person is to gain approval from people. He wants to look righteous, so people hold him in high regards. This is exactly what the Pharisees did. They did their alms in front of many people, disfigured their faces when fasting, loved to sit at the best seats in the synagogues, and enjoyed being called with pompous titles, just to name a few.

Sadly, they have their rewards. They have not waited for a far GREATER reward that only God can give them.

Here's food for thought:

When we do something good, we do it not to show how righteous we are, but instead, "We Do It To Show How Awesome The Living God Is". We do our good deeds so that people "may see [our] good works and glorify [our] Father in heaven" **(Matthew 5:16).**

Sign 6;
Self-Righteous People List Their Good Works

Have you ever noticed how hard it is for us to forget the good things we have done to other people? Every time we do something good, we have this little notepad in our brain where we list all our good deeds. Afterward, we add them all up and show ourselves and others how righteous we are!

Sometimes we think so highly of ourselves that we felt that God needs us so badly. Actually, the reverse is true: It is US who desperately need God!

When we do this, we forget that our righteousness is just like "Filthy Rugs" **(Isaiah 64:6).** Our righteousness pales down to nothing when compared to the righteousness of God.

In reality, it is not our job to list our good deeds. It is God's. "For God is not unrighteous to forget [our] work and labor of love, which [we] have shewed toward his name, in that [we] have ministered to the saints, and do minister" **(Hebrews 6:10).**

Sign 7;
Self-Righteous People Reject Correction.

If we remain self-righteous, time will come that it will make us callous. We hold on to our self-righteousness and it will harden us. And by the time when we need to be corrected, pride sets in, and we become unteachable.

This hardness of heart may spring from the belief that you know almost everything, that you already know what the scripture says, and nothing new can impress you anymore. You think that there's nothing to learn anymore and you won't let anybody tell you what to do. We have become too vain in our thinking that we won't allow anyone to point out where we might have got it wrong.

True righteous people possess a child-like attitude. That is entirely different to what self-righteous people feel about themselves. Jesus Christ was teachable in spite of His wisdom and divine nature. He did everything and anything His Father told Him to do.

Sign 8;
Self-Righteous People Talk Back To God

For God to work with self-righteous people, they need to be humbled first. However, self-righteousness may persist.

Like Job, we may talk back to God and rationalize our thoughts and actions. We may show God how rich, how we have increased in goods, and how we have need of nothing **(Revelation 3:17).** We may tell God how good we are by following His commandments and that He owes us a pat on the back and praises! However, just like the Laodicean church, we didn't know that we are actually "wretched, miserable, and poor, and blind, and naked" (same verse).

Sign 9;
Self-Righteous People Think Of Themselves As Important

Sometimes, in our zeal and passion in doing God's work, we fall into the trap of thinking that it's all about US.

We look at the results of our work and say, "Wow! Look how many people came into the church through me!" "Did you just see that? I just inspired the whole congregation with my sermon!" "Look at how much I am doing for the work of the church. I'm sure the church won't grow without me." "I pay a lot of tithes.

The pastor will surely miss me if I leave this church."

This type of thinking is focused on the self. Self-righteousness literally means "Self Right." In reality, we must all be "Christ-Right."

Sometimes we think so highly of ourselves that we felt that God needs us so badly. Actually, the reverse is true: It is us who desperately need God!

Righteous people don't think about the things they lost for following God. But rather, they concentrate on the things God gave them!

Sign 10;
Self-Righteous People Wallow In Self-Pity

Every time a self-righteous is chastened by God, he sulks in self-pity. Instead of seeing trials and challenges in life as a way to develop godly righteousness, they would instead pity and prevent themselves from developing the enthusiasm to fight back.

James said that we must "count it all joy when [we] fall into various trials." For a self-righteous person, he would just endure the trial and not actually rejoice in it. "We need to seecorrection as a way to bring us back to our loving father".

When God gives us a trial, it is not because He wants to prevent us from getting into the Kingdom, but to help us develop the righteousness that enables us to be part of His Family.

When we are corrected for our self-righteous arrogance, we must have a positive attitude, learn the lesson, and overcome. That's the only way we can destroy the shackles of self-righteousness that restrict our spiritual growth.

Sign 11;
A Self-Righteous Hypocrite Judges Others Based On Selective Standards, Not On All Of God's Word.

One of the most helpful chapters for understanding the sin of self-righteousness is Jesus' indictment of the Pharisees in **Matthew 23**. The Pharisees picked out certain parts of the Law and prided themselves on their obedience, but they neglected the weightier parts of the Law **(Matt. 23:23).** They tithed their table spices, but they neglected justice, mercy, and faithfulness. They invented loopholes around keeping the Law. They said that if you swore by the temple, you were not obligated to keep your word, but if you swore by the gold of the temple, you were obligated **(Matt. 23:16-21).** We laugh at how stupid that sounds, but many Christians do the same thing. God's Word tells us that God hates violence **(Ps. 11:5)** and that we should not even talk about immorality, impurity, or greed **(Eph. 5:3).** We should be innocent in what is evil **(Rom. 16:19).** But somehow it's okay to fill our minds with TV shows and movies that are filled with profanity, violence, and sexual immorality. The self-righteous person picks parts of the Bible that he likes and prides himself on keeping those parts. And he condemns as "legalists" those who seek to obey all of God's Word.

Sign 12;

A Self-Righteous Hypocrite Is More Concerned About External Conformity Than With True, Inner Godliness

Jesus said **(Matt. 23:28),** "So you, too, outwardly appear righteous to men, but inwardly you are full of hypocrisy and lawlessness." The Pharisees were concerned that they would not defile themselves for the Passover by going into Pilate's Gentile court **(John 18:28)** at the same time that they were seeking to crucify the innocent Lord Jesus! Self-righteous hypocrites want to keep up outward "Christian" appearances, but they don't judge their own sins on the heart level. They put on the happy Christian face at church, but use abusive speech with their families at home.

Sign 13;

A Self-Righteous Hypocrite Is Not Interested In Helping Others Grow In Godliness

Jesus said **(Matt. 23:13, 15),** "But woe to you, scribes and Pharisees, hypocrites, because you shut off the kingdom of heaven from people; for you do not enter in yourselves, nor do you allow those who are entering to go in…. Woe to you, scribes and Pharisees, hypocrites, because you travel around on sea and land to make one proselyte; and when he becomes one, you make him twice as much a son of hell as yourselves." They didn't care about the people or their hearts before God. They just wanted to gain followers so that they looked good.

The Difference Between Self-Righteous And Righteous

There are two ways to explain what righteous and self-righteous mean: the secular and the theological explanation. However, there are some stark differences here, with righteous people being painted overly positively when put into a more religious background.

Theological Perspective

In a sense, the polar opposite of sin in the Bible is righteousness. It describes the perfection that is God, and it's an essential attribute the only standard of living people should aim for if they want to stand before Him.

The thing with righteousness in the theological sense is that people are closely tied to sins and cannot become righteous on their own. Every notion that could make them appear more moral or holier than others is bound to self-righteous acts as the motivation behind them isn't to glorify Jesus. Therefore, only God can make someone righteous, or rather, Jesus assigned righteousness in people by atoning for their sins.Through the theological lens, self-righteousness is recognizing final authority to yourself and not God. Individuals who possess this trait are arrogant, smug, judgy, and much too confident in their own moral superiority. In contrast, the righteous are humble servants of God.

Secular Perspective

The secular perspective of self-righteous people doesn't paint it any better, as it once again implies smugness and narcissism. They are often greatly proud of their achievements (vainglorious), which makes them overly vain and can easily make others around them uncomfortable.

At the same time, they are hypocritical and enjoy double standards regarding their own behavior. They employ self-bias and judge others, believing their moral compass and enlightenment are always better than others.

Righteous people, on the other hand, are morally just and virtuous. They follow the rules and lead a good life, i.e., by not judging others, believing they are superior, etc.However, the irony here is that simply believing that righteous people are better could make someone self-righteous. To be truly righteous, you need to follow a moral code without comparing it to others or implying they should be more like you.

Final Thoughts

Is there even a truly righteous person in this world, or is the pursuit for that attribute flawed from the very start as humans are preoccupied with themselves? It is very likely!

Unless you are a religious person, you may never learn how to be righteous in the exact sense of the word. Whether you like it or not, self-righteousness seems to be a part of everyone's life to some extent. There's no doubt; it's hard to see the self righteousness in us. In fact, every time we do something good, the natural response is to have a certain amount of self-righteousness budding in our hearts.

However, if we truly see what we truly are without God, then we will realize that our righteousness must be from God. After all, it is Christ who lives in us, and it is Him who helps us produce the fruit of the Holy Spirit. Instead of building our own righteousness, we need to build the Righteousness of God. It is up to you to decide if you want to correct the behavior through making deeper connections, avoiding judgment, questioning your own beliefs and thoughts, and truly opening your mind.

This is a profound and significant subject we all need to think about. Self-righteousness is indeed a fatal sin that we all need to overcome, and by being alert to these deadly sins of self-righteousness, I hope we can be more successful in becoming less like us and be more like God!

Chapter five

Jesus Offers Escape from Hypocrisy

Once you're able to confess your sins to God, he is able to forgive us……The same with hypocrisy and this is going to be our main focus in this chapter. Before that, what are the dangers of living a Hypocrite's life?

5 Warnings for Hypocrites In The Church

If you've been in the church long enough, you start to notice a strange phenomenon. Some members of your congregation may speak godly words at church, then walk out the door and act completely differently in their real lives. You might have heard these people referred to as wolves in sheep's clothing. Put simply, they are hypocrites.

All of us are in danger of hypocrisy because we are all sinners. It is easy to slip and fall into human habits of sin… even when we are regular church-goers.

Jesus condemned the religious leaders of biblical times, "… honors me with their lips, but their heart is far from me; in vain do they worship me, teaching as doctrines the commandments of men." **(Matthew 15:8-9)**

But when we are true followers of Jesus Christ, we do not say one thing and do another. We must be on guard against this behavior in our own lives.

In a blog post, pastor and author Tim Challies writes that people who merely pretend to be godly should be warned of five things:

1. Hypocrisy Angers God.

Challies writes, "God hates hypocrisy and hypocrites… because hypocrisy misuses religion, taking advantage of its laws and decrees for self-advancement. The hypocrite wants religion—even the Christian faith—only for the advantages he gains from it."

God's laws are the only laws that Christians should be preaching. When we twist these around to meet our own desires, it angers God.

2. Hypocrisy Is Self-delusion.

"Many hypocrites deceive themselves, thinking that their hypocritical deeds are evidence of true godliness or, even worse, that they have the ability to merit God's favor," Challies says.

Acting hypocritically ultimately hurts yourself because you lose favor with God. Don't believe that hypocrisy is okay if it's not hurting anyone. It is hurting someone: you.

3. Hypocrisy Is Offensive To God And Man.

"Unbelievers hate the hypocrite because he makes himself appear godly; God hates him because he merely looks godly," writes Challies.

No one finds hypocrisy to be an attractive quality. Not God, not the world. You don't want to become everyone's enemy.

4. Hypocrisy Is Pointless.

Challies says, "The hypocrite may labor hard in this life, but as soon as he dies he will lose absolutely everything. The only reward he will be able to enjoy will be in this life since he will certainly be condemned to death."

What is the point in pretending to be godly when it ends in eternal damnation? Sinners will not inherit the kingdom of God **(Galatians 5:19-21).** Genuine believers who have accepted Christ will.

5. Hypocrisy Brings No Comfort In Death.

"People who have only painted over their depravity with a thin veneer of counterfeit holiness will find themselves without hope and without comfort upon their deathbed," writes Challies.

A life of false Christianity is not one of happiness. A life lived in holiness is what one can look back on without regrets.

How can the hypocrite save himself from a life of sin? Scripture says clearly: Repent.

Tim Challies writes, "... there is hope for the hypocrite and the words of Paul should ring in the ears of the hypocrite: 'Do you presume on the riches of his kindness and forbearance and patience, not knowing that God's kindness is meant to lead you to repentance?' **(Romans 2:4).** Those who turn to Christ in repentance and faith will be cleansed of every sin, including this one."

And if you are living a holy life, what can you do to keep hypocrites from making you stumble in your own faith?

Crosswalk.com contributor Debbie McDaniel writes, "The best way to expose the false lies of the enemy is to know the Truth of the One voice who matters most. Know the real and you'll know what is false… As we keep pressing in to know God, who is real, who is Truth, and we set our minds on His Word, spending time there, meditating on it, eventually we become very trained in detecting the 'fake'.

Dangers of Hypocrisy

Then spake Jesus to the multitude, and to his disciples, Saying, The scribes and the Pharisees sit in Moses' seat: All therefore whatsoever they bid you observe, that observe and do; but do not ye after their works: for they say, and do not. For they bind heavy burdens and grievous to be borne, and lay them on men's shoulders; but they themselves will not move them with one of their fingers." **(Matthew 23:1-4)**

In one of their humorous true life story collections, Reader's Digest told about a lady named Callie Rough who was arrested in Middletown, Ohio for shoplifting at a local Dollar General store. To make matters worse, she had two young children with her as she stole from the store. To top off the situation, among the things which she stole was a book: 101 Ways to Be a Great Mom.

The religious leaders of Jesus' day made a great show of public righteousness. They offered loud public prayers, sounded trumpets to make sure people were paying attention when they gave, and spent a great deal of time telling other people how to live. The reason they hated Jesus so much was that He exposed their hypocrisy. They said the right things, but they did not live them. Hypocrisy is bad enough in its own right, but it also makes us resistant to the call of God to repent. When we are living hypocritically, we can justify ourselves to ourselves (though God is never fooled) by pointing to the outward expressions while ignoring the evil in our hearts. When we think of ourselves as righteous, we see no need to change our ways. Jesus saw this in the Pharisees, and revealed it, but they rejected His message. "And he spake this parable unto certain which trusted in themselves that they were righteous, and despised others" **(Luke 18:9).** They were content if people viewed them as doing right, without regard to whether they actually were

The world is full of hypocrites, and many people are trying to live a double life. Such kind of life is suited only for two-faced, a fictional supervillain who tormented Gotham city and had to be stopped by Batman. According to the early 13th century definition, hypocrisy is referred to as the claim or pretense of having beliefs, standards, qualities, behaviors, virtues, motivations, etc which one does not actually possess.

The unfortunate part is seeing this lifestyle lived in the body of Christ. If it is any type of life, hypocrisy is the worst kind of life to ever exist. Those who do so risk losing themselves in the process. The Bible has had a lot to say about this topic, it is full of warnings against hypocrites; Jesus pronounced seven different judgments against the scribes and Pharisees because of the same vice **(Matthew 23:1-36).**

Apostle Paul had to confront Peter over living a "two-face" life. The encounter between Peter and Paul gives us four things that help in understanding the danger of hypocrisy and why believers should stay clear from it. There are four dangers of Hypocrisy which can be considered from this passage:

1. Hypocrisy makes you live a Double Life

Peter had no problem sharing life with the Gentile believers in Antioch until his fellow Jews arrived. He did not want the Jews to know and see him associating with the Gentiles. Peter was living a double life,the Gentiles' way of life, and the Jewish strict way of living. He was switching hats of whatever favored his circumstance and Paul had to rebuke him. James wrote in his letter, "A double minded person is unstable in all his ways" **(James 1:8)**

Hypocrisy is among the list of things for us to put away if we are going to grow in Salvation **(1 Peter 2:1).** I guess the question is, what kind of life are you living? Are there things you are hiding? Are there certain hats you put on to make yourself comfortable, but you would not want those who really know you to find you wearing? "The only people who are mad at you for speaking the truth are those people who are living a lie. Keep speaking the truth."

2. Hypocrisy makes you live in Fear

There is an interesting word of wisdom from the book of Proverbs. It says, "The fear of man lays a snare, but whoever trusts in the LORD is safe" **(Proverbs 29:25)**. Peter had allowed the opinions of his fellow Jews grip him so tightly that he could not enjoy the freedom Christ had given. Peter could not proclaim before his fellow Jews the great things God had done among the Gentiles, and why was that? It's because he was afraid.

He was afraid people would discover his pretentious life, he was afraid his fellow Jews would not accept him again. He was afraid so he had to withdraw from his brothers and sisters in Christ, those who shared the same bond of love like the brothers from Jerusalem he was afraid of. Living a hypocritical life makes us miss out on what God has to offer for those who are free in Christ. Jesus in speaking to his disciples about fear said, "And do not fear those who kill the body but cannot kill the soul. Rather, fear him who can destroy both soul and body in hell" **(Matthew 10:28).**

Is it not true that we have our fears misplaced most of the time ? Let me ask a question, Who has your fears? I think we so often live in so much fear of man than we are of God. "If we feel we have to change our Christian beliefs to match those of our companions, we are on dangerous grounds."

Compromise is an important element in getting along with others, but we should never compromise the truth of God's Word. The Word of God should be a "Non-Negotiable" non-debatable thing. If you are beginning to debate whether to believe the Bible or not, whether you should obey God's Word or man then it is time you checked your biblical conviction because, "We must obey God rather than men" **(Acts 5:29).**

3. Hypocrisy leads others astray

"And the rest of the Jews acted hypocritically along with him, so that even Barnabas was led astray by their hypocrisy." We need to be watchful how we live, our action might either draw people to Christ or push them away. Just imagine, that even Barnabas was led astray.

This guy was a mature believer, he is the one who took Paul in when all were afraid of him; he is the man we hear the Holy Spirit saying, "Set apart for me Barnabas and Saul for the work to which I called them" **(Acts 13:2).** If Barnabas was led astray because certain believers were acting hypocritically, how many more people were probably led astray? If we are living this way, how many people might end up being led astray because of our lifestyle?

We preach the gospel not just by the words that come out of our mouth, but much more by how we live out the truth we profess. May a soul never be lost to hell because we were living as hypocrites. "…let your light shine before others, so that they may see your good works and give glory to your father in Heaven" – **(Matthew 5:16).**

4. Hypocrisy makes you live contrary to the Gospel

"But when I saw that their conduct was not in step with the truth of the Gospel,.." In their attempt to please both sides (the Gentiles and

Jews) and live for themselves, Peter and some of his fellow Jews had wandered off from the truth. This is how easy it is to drift from the truth of the Scripture.

It begins with one lie, one compromise, one pretense, one twisted Scripture, and before you know it, it has become a way of life. May we constantly check ourselves, constantly soak ourselves in the Word of God, but much more allow the truth we already know to bring the change God intends to bring in our lives.

"You cannot live the life you want, when you want, and how you want it, and still be in line with the Gospel." Peter learned his lesson the hard way, but the greatest thing about his life was that he was a repentant man, he was a man who listened. He later on wrote to believers who were scattered throughout Asia Minor about spiritual growth and the danger that poses a threat to it.

He includes hypocrisy among the things believers should put away from their lives. He writes, "So put away all malice and all deceit and hypocrisy and envy and all slander. Like newborn infants, long for the pure spiritual milk, that by it you may grow into salvation, If you indeed have tasted that the Lord is Good" **(1 Peter 2:1 – 3).**

Hypocrisy is dangerous because it hides the truth from people seeking it. As a result, it makes people believe in a lie because they who live to please the flesh live contrary to the Gospel. Let's be mindful of how we live on this earth because believe it or not, you are causing an impact on people's lives. Only, be sure you are causing a positive impact; an impact that is turning sinners into saints because they are drawn to Jesus Christ. Let us stop pretending and be real.

The Hypocrisy Of An Undeserved Reputation

It is true that "a good name is to be chosen rather than great riches" **(Proverbs 22:1).** But that is only true to the extent that our good name, our reputation, accurately represents who we are. If we cultivate and promote a reputation for ourselves that is better than we actually are, God has a scathing term for us: hypocrite.

And hypocrisy includes maintaining and promoting a reputation that we once deserved but now do not. The Christians in Sardis had a reputation for being alive because once they had been. That's why Jesus told them to "strengthen what remains and is about to die" **(Revelation 3:2).** They used to have life, but it was dying.

Why did they need this rebuke? Didn't they notice their spiritual decline? Didn't they discern their hypocrisy? Well, if they were anything like me, they probably did to some degree. But there is something powerfully deceptive about a reputation. We can easily be deceived into thinking that if others see us as "alive," then perhaps it's true.

Smoke and Mirrors

As a result of the fall, each one of us suffers from a sin-induced dissociative identity disorder. Our sin natures rebelliously dissociate our identities as dependent creatures, branches that are designed to joyfully, trustingly abide in our Creator-Vine **(John 15:5),** preferring to think of ourselves as creators-vines. But having unhinged our identities from our Creator, we lose our grip on reality who we really are.

So to compensate, we try to stitch our identities together with chosen pieces of our own aspirations and the cumulative total of other people's perceptions of us and our reputation. We use this reputation as a mirror to reflect to us who we are, and to project an image of ourselves that we want others to see.

But such an identity really is only smoke and mirrors. Our self-perception and other people's perception of us do not reflect or project accurately who we are. They are misleading images because they are in large part imaginations.

We aren't who we want to think we are or who other people think we are. All we truly are is who we are before God.

Jesus Provides The Escape From Hypocrisy

The hypocritical life, the smoke and mirrors life of inhabiting an undeserved reputation, is a trap.

It can be a deluding trap that deadens our awareness that real spiritual vitality is ebbing away. It can also be a trap of pride. We may be aware that the social currency of our reputation is highly inflated, but the price of admission to that reality may appear more than we are willing to pay.

But into our blinding, impoverishing Sardisian pride comes Jesus, speaking words that at first sting badly, but in truth are full of grace: "I know your works" **(Revelation 3:1).** He knows. He knows who and what we really are. Before him we are fully exposed **(Hebrews 4:13).**

And that is very good news, because Jesus provides the escape from the guilt, power, and identity-confusion of hypocrisy that we so desperately need. He is our Creator-Vine, our source and the source of our real identity **(1 Corinthians 1:30).** And he is full of grace **(John 1:14),** having died for us while we were yet sinners **(Romans 5:8),** fully paying the debt of every sin **(Colossians 2:14),** and offering complete forgiveness if we repent **(1 John 1:9).** His rebukes, if heeded, always lead us out of sin's captivity to abundant life **(John 10:10).**

And from his word to the Sardis church, here is the escape from hypocrisy Jesus offers us: "Remember, then, what you received and heard. Keep it, and repent." **(Revelation 3:3)** Do not waste any more of your life playing with smoke and mirrors. Do not be content with a phantom reputation of past zeal and achievements. Remember what you received from Jesus; remember his word **(John 15:7).** Repent of hypocrisy; come clean to Jesus, and anyone else if necessary. Keep his word. Pursue the joyful, humble life of an abiding branch, and you will bear much fruit **(John 15:5).**

The reward is great for those who receive Jesus's offer of escape: "The one who conquers will be clothed thus in white garments, and I will never blot his name out of the book of life. I will confess his name before my Father and before his angels." **(Revelation 3:5)** Let us hear what the Spirit is saying.

The church in Sardis seems to have listened to the Spirit. In the 2nd century the church was known as a bastion of doctrinal fidelity and bold defense of the faith and a church remained there until the 14th century.

Are You a Hypocrite, or Someone Who Struggles with Sin?

In **(Matthew 12:31),** Jesus said, "Therefore I say to you, every sin and blasphemy will be forgiven men, but the blasphemy against the Spirit will not be forgiven men." If a person continues to ignore and reject the call to repent and believe in God, that is blasphemy against the Spirit. One who dies in this state has committed the unpardonable sin. If you are reading this, you may be in the process of committing it, but there is hope.

The religious leaders of Jesus' day were attributing the works of God to Satan - this was reflected in their heart...the fruit of their life.

Jesus continued in **(Matthew 12:33-34),** "For a tree is known by its fruit. Brood of vipers! How can you, being evil, speak good things? For out of the abundance of the heart the mouth speaks." How is this relevant for you today? Would Jesus have said the same things to you?

Religious people often say "good things," but their hearts deliberately disobey. This is called religious hypocrisy; God hates it. This is much different than a believer who struggles with sin. A religious person acts religious but doesn't know God.

Around the globe, millions have religion but not a true relationship. Jesus states, "These people draw near to Me with their mouth, and honor Me with their lips, but their heart is far from Me" **(Matthew 15:8).** "Millions of professed believers talk as if [Christ] were real and act as if He were not. And always our actual position is to be discovered by the way we act, not by the way we talk." Is this where you find yourself today?

The only way to awaken those who are spiritually dead is with words that confront. Jesus used cutting words to spark change: "Brood of vipers." Sometimes, we are to do the same, primarily when preaching.

Pastors...did you catch that? God doesn't just want us to encourage; He wants us to confront. Many go to church sporadically, but would rather sit at home. They are disengaged and bored during worship when they do attend. Their social media posts resemble Hollywood not the work of the Spirit. They choose friends who complement their worldly lifestyle, rather than friends who challenge them to live for God. They look forward to consuming alcohol, and avoid prayer and Bible study. The things of the world are exciting and the things of God are dull.

Their movie and video choices look no different than what the culture promotes. Their conversations at work include every topic except God, and at home, their words are shallow and lifeless. Their waking thoughts are focused on wealth, pleasure, or entertainment. They have religion, but not a genuine relationship. Sadly, many churches are encouraging this lifestyle rather than confronting it.

This spiritual climate is where the majority of religious people live. Floyd Mayweather wrote recently on Instagram, "Yes, I got a 14 passenger jet. Got to give them another reason to hate, but I will motivate the people that are ambitious and want to be winners in life. I am guilty! I'm materialistic and I'm motivated by money...but God is first in my life." It's impossible to love the things of this world and still have God as a "priority."

Granted, there is a huge difference between a hypocrite and someone who is struggling in their relationship with God. We all struggle, but hypocrites play a role, much like an actor. They are deceiving people by saying one thing and doing another. Those who are unrepentant and indulge in sin are outside of God's will...outside of salvation. Those who are struggling turn to God and allow Him to cleanse and redeem.

God's Response to Hypocrisy

Kindness and Judgment

Hypocrites Who Give Christianity a Bad Name

You can almost see the religious types over in the corner as this is read, feeling very smug and self-righteous, and thinking "We don't hate God; we're not full of murder and strife and wickedness and evil schemes." It's this kind of person who sometimes gives Christianity a very bad name. Many go to Christian churches and are not true Christians.

If you have ever blamed Christianity for that kind of hypocrisy, you will see in these next verses what God's response to hypocrisy is, and that you will make up your mind about God and Christ and his way of salvation not mainly on the basis of what some religious people are like, but on the basis of what God is like.

Two Responses To Hypocrisy

Here's what Paul says about these finger-pointing people who are smug in their own sense of righteousness **(Romans 2:1–5).** Of all the things we could focus on in these verses I want us to see two main things: Two responses of God to hypocrisy.

Therefore you have no excuse, every one of you who passes judgment, for in that which you judge another, you condemn yourself; for you who judge practice the same things. And we know that the judgment of God rightly falls upon those who practice such things. But do you suppose this, O man, when you pass judgment on those who practice such things, and do the same yourself, that you will escape the judgment of God? Or do you think lightly of the riches of his kindness and tolerance and patience, not knowing that the kindness of God leads you to repentance? But because of your stubbornness and unrepentant heart you are storing up wrath for yourself on the day of wrath and revelation of the righteous judgment of God.

Now all those phrases tell us two things about God. It tells us that God is kind and that God is just. God is kind and God is just. Let's just look for a minute at each of these two attributes of God.

God Is Just

God is just. When Paul says to the hypocrites in the first verse, "You have no excuse," he shows God's concern with justice. If these people had a legitimate excuse for their sins of judgmentalism and hypocrisy, God would be unjust to judge them. But the whole point of this passage is to do exactly what we saw Paul doing in Romans 1:20 and 32 in regard to the Gentiles. He wants to show that they are without excuse. In other words, when judgment comes from God because of sin, it will not be unjust. No one will be able to raise any legitimate objection.

So the first thing to learn about God and his response to hypocrisy is that God is just, and his just judgment is coming not only on the so-called pagan people who live in sin, but also on the moral and religious people who disdain the pagan people, while doing many things that show they don't trust and love God. That list in 1:29–31 includes things like greed, envy, gossip, unloving, unmerciful. Has any of us been as merciful and loving toward others as he or she ought to be?

God Is Kind

But the second thing this text tells us about God and about his response to hypocrites is that God is kind. In fact, you will notice in verse 4 that Paul speaks of the "riches of his kindness." That means that he is not just a little bit kind, but that he has huge resources of kindness to pour out on us. In fact, he is pouring them out on us all right now.

"The eternal life of everyone depends on the kindness of God, not our goodness."
Isn't that the implication of the other two words Paul uses to describe God's kindness? He uses the words "forbearance" and "patience." In other words, God's justice does not demand that he punish us for our sins immediately. But his kindness leads him to forbear and to be patient with us. That word "patience" in the original Greek (the language Paul wrote in) is just like the English word "longsuffering." It means that God may endure months and years and decades of our stubbornness and resistance to repentance.

The very fact that any of us is alive today is owing to this great kindness of God. He could have been done with us many years ago and taken us away to judgment. But here we are. And this should amaze us. Thursday is Thanksgiving. And today is a Thanksgiving Celebration. And oh, how thankful we should be for the riches of God's kindness, and for his forbearance and patience. We are alive. We are present under the proclamation of his gospel. And we have this clear word from **(Romans 2:4):** "The kindness of God leads you to repentance."

Depend on God's Kindness
That is my prayer this morning. That everyone here will be sure you have repented and are now trusting in Jesus Christ for forgiveness and for the gift of God's righteousness. It doesn't matter if you are an irreligious secularist or a moralistic critic of others. The eternal life of everyone in this room depends on the kindness of God not our goodness. And the issue is not whether you have been baptized, or whether you belong to a church, or whether you have walked an aisle, or prayed a prayer, or signed a card. None of those things saves.

What God leads you to is repentance, which means that you have a profound change of mind and heart so that you hate sin and hate hypocrisy and turn to Jesus in humility and faith and say, "You are my only hope." And trust him for all the promises of forgiveness and help and life that he bought when he died. They belong freely to everyone who believes in him.

Finding Forgiveness for Religious Hypocrisy **(Isaiah 6:1-8)**

Isaiah, a man in ministry, spent many years thinking the same thing. As God's mouth-piece, Isaiah did all the external action of calling Israel to repentance. He was a "man of God"; he was calling people to repentance; he did everything external to please God. Did you know he was also a hypocrite?

Look at Isaiah 6, chapters after Isaiah's beginning of ministry. In this passage, Isaiah becomes face-to-face with the LORD Himself, Isaiah comes into the presence of this holy and righteous God. How does Isaiah respond? "Woe is me for I am ruined because I am a man of unclean lips and live among a people of unclean lips, and because my eyes have seen the King, the LORD of Armies" **(Isaiah 6:5).** Isaiah was a religious hypocrite; he saw his sin of hypocrisy before anyone else. Even biblical writers could go through the motions, forgetting the absolute holiness and glory of our Lord.

And yet, it is this same glory of God that turns
Isaiah from his sin, because the next verse
promises Isaiah that "your iniquity [i.e. evil
action] is removed and your sin is atoned for
[i.e. forgiven]". Isaiah is not left despondent in
guilt and shame; he is forgiven so that he can
return to God again in loving obedience !
You yourself may have experienced an Isaiah-
moment, where you see the infinite magnitude
of God's glory and holiness, and you tell
yourself: "God, I'm unworthy. I'm too guilty!"
Yet our conviction is only the first step; God
offers us so much more than just therapy for
feeling bad about ourselves. He forgives that
guilt of religious hypocrisy, going through the
motions of "church" instead of daily coming to
God in utter dependence.
You might feel like a hypocrite today; don't
worry, it's you and me both. Praise God who
offers us something so much more in Jesus
Christ. Instead of only Isaiah seeing the glory of
God, Jesus "became flesh and dwelt among us.
We observed his glory, the glory as the one and
only Son from the Father, full of grace and
truth" **(John 1:14).** Christ himself came in the
flesh, and so often the presence of Christ alone
is enough for people to fall at their feet and seek

forgiveness. Thankfully, Christ came to live the perfect life in our place, died as the perfect sacrifice, and was raised again through the power of God. And it's based on that fact alone that we can walk in the newness of life today. If you're suffering from complacency, if you're suffering from "faking Christianity," if you feel the weight of guilt and shame, you can bring all of this to Jesus' feet. The absolute glory of Christ's death and resurrection for us will always be enough to cure us from religious hypocrisy.

Conclusion

Hypocrisy is among the greatest sins of Christians all throughout the ages. It has led many astray. Due to hypocrisy, many unbelievers are turned off to Christianity, thinking that we are no different to others. Sadly, hypocrisy isn't just found among members of the Church, but also among its leaders. We have all been hypocrites at some time of our lives. In fact, this sin is a struggle for many of us.

Now, here's the hope that we all have: hypocrisy, like any sin, can be overcome. You may not successfully eliminate it from your life overnight, but the important thing is that you are struggling against it.

To the degree that this becomes real for us, and is more than words on the page of a book, or inferential knowledge based only on what others have said, to the degree that this is a real experience for us, we start to climb off the stage. We are less the actor (the hypocrite) and more the authentic self God has created us to be. We begin to lose our obsession with what others think of us. We are less desperate for

their approval. It is not that we become
sociopaths caring not one whit what others
think. We still groom ourselves etc., but we are
not obsessed with the good opinion of others. It
is enough that we know our heavenly Father
and his love for us.

Hence, hypocrisy, at least as Jesus teaches it
here. is a richer concept than we often think of
today. To this sad and poignant problem, Jesus
addresses a very powerful and personal solution
of knowing "your heavenly Father" and
experiencing his love for you. As long as you
are putting an effort in eliminating hypocrisy in
your life even little by little, God can see your
heart and will commend you for that. He is
more than willing to help you overcome
hypocrisy and live a genuine and blessed life.
Just pray and ask for His help.No one's perfect
but we must aim for perfection **(Matthew
5:48).** That's how high God has set the standard
that we all should live by.

With these guides, I believe you will have a
clearer picture of what hypocrisy is all about
and why God shuns it. And by having this fresh
insight, you will have a better idea on how to

overcome this.May we be consistent people, honest about our continuing corruption but also honestly living in the work of Christ. Amen.

www.ingramcontent.com/pod-product-compliance
Lightning Source LLC
Chambersburg PA
CBHW061528120726
48001CB00004B/1437